ADVANCE PRAISE FOR *IF ONLY LOVE*

"Achingly beautiful. Exquisite writing, a skillful structuring, the weight of sadness laced with the lightness of a burning love and a boundless spirit. An intensely personal journey that also wends through many worlds. I knew Shelley Saywell's book would be wonderful. This is a gift."

—Lyse Doucet, BBC's Chief international correspondent and author of *The Finest Hotel in Kabul*

"Shelley Saywell's poignant, hauntingly beautiful memoir takes us on an epic journey of resilience and regret that will at once break your heart and give you hope in the enduring power and endless possibility of love."

—Mellissa Fung, author of *Under an Afghan Sky* and *Between Good and Evil*

"A heartbreaking memoir of love lost, love found and then lost again. Shelley Saywell, the accomplished creator of documentary films, reveals another part of herself—a tender heart and the joy and grief that accompany deep passion. Even through the pain, she shows that over time profound love is completely worth the risk."

—Antanas Sileika, author of *Some Unfinished Business*

"In this miracle of a story, Saywell interweaves two strands of profound human experience, at opposing ends of the emotional spectrum: falling in love and grieving the premature death of a life partner. In the hands of a master storyteller, this seemingly incompatible double helix soars into a triumph of the heart. A transcontinental journey of hope, and serendipity, *If Only Love* is a book for anyone who has ever dreamt of a second chance."

—Roxana Spicer, author of *The Traitor's Daughter*

"Exquisite. *If Only Love* abounds in sensorial richness, startlingly fresh phrasings, and Saywell's incomparable, expansive spirit. If you've ever loved anyone, this deftly crafted Möbius strip of a book will have you reconsidering the way you live."

—Barbara Tran, author of *Precedented Parroting*, nominated for the Governor General's Literary Award for Poetry

"*If Only Love* is an epic true story of a great love lost in youth and rekindled decades later, only to be wrenched away again. It is a beautiful, sometimes painful and always inspiring tribute to everlasting love. It took my breath away and made me look into my own heart."

—Anna Maria Tremonti, broadcast journalist and creator of the podcast, *Welcome to Paradise*

If Only Love

If Only Love

A memoir of second chances

Shelley Saywell

Random House Canada

PUBLISHED BY RANDOM HOUSE CANADA

 Published in 2026 by Random House Canada, a division of Penguin Random House Canada Limited, Toronto.

Random House Canada, an imprint of Penguin Random House Canada Limited
320 Front Street West, Suite 1400
Toronto, Ontario, M5V 3B6, Canada
penguinrandomhouse.ca

Random House Canada and colophon are registered trademarks of Penguin Random House LLC.

The authorized representative in the EU for product safety and compliance is Penguin Random House Ireland, Morrison Chambers, 32 Nassau Street, Dublin D02 YH68, Ireland. https://eu-contact.penguin.ie

LIBRARY AND ARCHIVES CANADA CATALOGUING IN PUBLICATION
Title: If only love: a memoir of second chances / Shelley Saywell.
Names: Saywell, Shelley, author.
Identifiers: Canadiana (print) 20250207583 | Canadiana (ebook) 20250208016 | ISBN 9781039013711 (softcover) | ISBN 9781039013728 (EPUB)
Subjects: LCSH: Saywell, Shelley—Marriage. | LCSH: Cancer—Patients—Family relationships—Biography. | LCSH: Spouses—Canada—Biography. | LCSH: Love. | LCSH: Marriage. | LCSH: Loss (Psychology) | LCSH: Motion picture producers and directors—Canada—Biography. | LCGFT: Autobiographies.
Classification: LCC HQ560 .S29 2026 | DDC 306.872092—dc23

Text design: Lisa Jager
Cover design: Lisa Jager
Image credits: Courtesy of the author, with special thanks to Mark Ashida for the photo of Shelley Saywell and Daniel Peterson on the train in Japan
Additional cover texture: autsawin / Getty Images
Typesetting: Erin Cooper

Printed in Canada

10 9 8 7 6 5 4 3 2 1

For Pete, my first love

and Daniel, my ever after

Once, far over the breakers

I caught a glimpse

Of a white bird

And fell in love

With this dream which obsesses me

—YOSANO AKIKO

Contents

Before

THE BOY SITS cross-legged in a kimono, dark hair and round eyes. He is listening to a story. It might be about a samurai warrior defending Kochi Castle. It might be about the way the firebombs flamed when they descended on the city.

Now he is dressed in a child's cowboy suit, hat dangling from strings down his back. He is tall for his age, standing with legs spread and hands at hips, ready to outdraw his opponent. The cowboy suit has just arrived in Japan, in a brown paper parcel postmarked North Carolina.

He's a quiet child. His words, when they come, might be in English or Japanese. He watches his father writing a sermon in the next room, while his mother is at the piano leading her Bible class in song. It's raining in slashes so straight and wide he can see each line; the typhoon season has trapped him inside. He wants to be climbing trees or riding his bicycle along the ocean towards the castle walls. He wants to be with his friends, not in this house that is different from the rest, home to the family of foreigners.

The city where they live still bears the marks of war, the charred ruins left by a thousand tons of incendiary bombs dropped by his American countrymen, ordered by U.S. Bomber Command. It's on the far shore of Shikoku, a southern island of Japan. This is the place he thinks of as home. This is the land where he was born.

The girl leans against the giant sequoia, peering up at the towering tree. Her grandmother snaps a photograph. She is visiting Vancouver Island, birthplace of her parents, home of her grandparents, a place of loggers at the edge of North America. Later she will collect shells and starfish and put them in a bucket, clambering over the rocky beach before the incoming tide covers the pebbles and sand.

Look. She shields her eyes and squints. The sun dances on the waves, making shapes that look like swimmers, then whales. The vastness of the ocean reaches into her imagination and takes her to faraway lands.

The Japanese accept this boy, child of their former enemies. They invite him into their homes and permit him to attend primary school with their children. He pulls his cap down over his hair, to try to disguise his difference. He is not a "volunteer," the name his grandmother gives to flowers that grow unbidden in the garden; he is not like his parents, hoping to transplant their faith. He is something never seen here before. He has emerged from this soil, a wildflower.

Now he has turned thirteen and is travelling to boarding school on the overnight ferry to Kobe. He is beginning to learn that home is elusive, that he will spend his life searching for a place to belong. He watches the waves swell and fall as the vessel plows through the open sea.

The girl has crossed the ocean.

She leans on the rail of the Star Ferry, looking out at the Hong Kong harbour. American warships and Chinese junks blast their approach; fishermen in sampans pole against the wake of cruise liners. The smells of fish and fuel and sweat and sandalwood waft through the salt air. Her hair whips around her face and her ears sting and bleed, newly pierced in a rite of adolescence. She is about to turn thirteen.

She tries not to stare when she sees them, the couple at the far end of the deck, locked in an embrace. She lets out a sigh, desperate to be older, to be like them.

Below, the waters churn and her senses awaken. He is somewhere close and she is coming to him.

Phone Call

DANIEL WAS LYING with his head in my lap. I traced the lines of his eyebrows, his cheekbones and jaw, feeling my way over the shapes and planes, the soft and rough surfaces I knew so well.

I loved to study his face.

In the years we were apart, I had often tried to picture it, wondering how it had changed from the face of a teenager into a man's. When I finally saw him again after almost three decades, I shook my head and laughed. His eyes were the same as I remembered, a shifting hazel colour. The indent in his cheek when he smiled still had the power to slay me.

After twelve years of marriage I still snuck sideways glances at him, just to reassure myself. Yes, he was really here. Yes, it was really him. I wanted to know what he was thinking, loved the sound of his laughter, was set on fire by his touch. But staring at his face was my favourite thing. It was like looking into a deep well, his eyes pools of grey or jade green.

I stroked his beard with its flecks of grey, then traced his bottom lip.

"I wish you were coming with me."

"Me too," he sighed.

I was leaving for Italy. Daniel had encouraged me to go, to take a break after completing two documentary films back-to-back, one on domestic violence, the other on homeless musicians. He was returning to his rented condo in Washington, D.C., where he was part of a conservation team restoring murals painted by Constantino Brumidi in the 1800s to adorn the ceilings and hallways of the United States Senate. While the lawmakers were in recess during August, there would be fewer restrictions to working on site, and they could push towards their next deadline. For the past few years, the Brumidi Corridors had been more of a companion to him than I was, and though we had promised we would meet every three weeks, in D.C. or in our house in Toronto, deadlines too often kept us apart.

We were lounging around, listening to music, feeling a little blue because one of our infrequent weeks together was coming to an end. "All You Need Is Love" by the Beatles came up on the playlist. Daniel mimicked the trumpet notes through closed lips.

Love, love, love.

"I read somewhere that Paul and Linda McCartney never spent a night apart in all the years of their marriage." I made a long face.

"I know." Daniel let out a sigh.

"If we aren't careful, we'll piss off the gods who reunited us."

His laughter turned to a moan. "Don't make me laugh, it hurts too much." He had slipped on a scaffold and thrown out his back, and it didn't seem to be getting better.

"Please get an X-ray when you get to D.C."

He sat up and wrapped his arms around me, pressing his lips to my ear. "I will. And don't worry, I promise I'll come with you on holiday next time."

In Rome I checked into my hotel and called Daniel, but he didn't answer. I left a message, then sent a text. The next morning I took a train to Tuscany. My brother Jim and his husband, Keith, picked me up at the station. We drove past fields of sunflowers and olive groves and distant stone villages that had looked the same for five hundred years.

"Welcome to Pieve," my brother said as we pulled up outside the sixteenth-century stone house he'd bought for a song when he was teaching architecture in Florence years before. He and Keith lived in Hong Kong, but every August they came back here to cook and paint and restore themselves.

I left my phone on the bedside table to charge, then joined them on the terrace overlooking the garden and raised a glass to missing family and friends.

"Daniel would adore this," I said. "Too bad he has to work on the murals of an Italian master instead of enjoying *la dolce vita*."

× × ×

The next afternoon, the Tuscan sun was burning hot, scorching the garden. We went inside to take a siesta in the cool stone rooms. I chose a novel from the bookshelf and settled into the sofa.

The phone rang.

"That's strange," said my brother. "No one ever calls on the landline."

He picked it up. "*Pronto.*"

I felt my stomach drop. My brother was listening to someone but looking at me.

"It's Daniel," Jim said, handing me the phone. He and Keith left the room to give me privacy.

"Honey, I'm sorry, I must have left my cellphone off. How did you get this number?" I asked without taking a breath.

Daniel's voice was muffled, hard to make out. "This is a call I never wanted to make," I thought I heard him say.

A thousand black birds clawed at my scalp, flapping their wings against my ears. "What's happened?"

"I fainted from pain, went to emergency . . . had an MRI . . . they want to admit me." He began to sob. I had never heard Daniel cry.

Something takes over when the brain can't register. I've noticed this while making documentaries in conflict zones, seeing people in unimaginable situations slip into automatic mode. My mind was shuttering, blocking fear, focused on the practical. We didn't have health coverage in the United States. We both had to get home.

"I'm going to hang up now," I said. "I'll call my dad and ask him to book us flights to Toronto. It's too hard from here—the internet is sketchy. Keep your phone on."

"I'm sorry, I'm sorry," he was saying.

"No, baby, don't say that. Soon we'll be together, and we'll figure everything out."

Jim and Keith drove me back to the station. The scenery moved in reverse past the train window. Back in Rome, I checked into the hotel I'd left two days earlier, to wait for my flight in the morning.

I needed to get some air.

The streets surrounding the Spanish Steps were thick with end-of-summer crowds moving in slow motion, lethargic in the heat. Next to the fountain, across from the house where the poet Keats had died, a busker was singing "Hotel California" off-key. Time seemed inverted, collapsed, strange. Children slurped gelato as it dripped down from small plastic cups onto sticky fingers and melted on the uneven cobblestones beneath my feet. Against the sky, three lone palm trees wavered like a mirage.

I moved aimlessly, my mind splintered like the patterns of late-day sun refracted off shop windows. I found myself staring at a display of lingerie in pale blue lace.

Daniel would love it if I surprised him by wearing something like that, I thought. Then I was in the boutique, fishing out my credit card, paying the exorbitant price. *Everything will be okay*, I told myself, clutching the bag with its fancy logo.

Outside, the crowds carried me along the busy shopping street until I stopped dead, forcing a stream of people to fork around me. How could this be happening after everything we'd been through, after all the years apart?

In the hotel room I rested my head on the pillow, knowing there would be no sleep. The air conditioner made a whirring noise like an old movie projector, and a filmstrip of memories played in my head.

There he was, a boy of seventeen, moving across the green towards me. He grinned, revealing a small gap between his front teeth. I was arguing a point, acting contrary to hold his attention, until he put a finger to my lips and said, "Hush."

The scenes flickered and flashed through the decades until I reached the last one. He was heading out the front door to go to the airport. I called him back, demanding one last hug. He opened his arms and smiled, but he was pale, and dark smudges circled his eyes. Why hadn't I noticed?

I turned on the light, the words he'd said on the phone finally sinking in.

"They think it might be cancer."

My mind cast around, searching for something, anything to hold on to. It flew through a myriad of terrifying scenarios until, like a homing bird, it returned to a safe place, my fixed point.

We had imprinted at seventeen. Whatever happened, we had already proved that love can defy time.

Dream

TEN MONTHS LATER, the dream wakes me before dawn. I was chasing someone, calling out to please wait. The figure I pursued kept moving away, until it morphed into a charcoal drawing. The drawing broke into slashes, which became words. I tried to read them, but the letters faded until there was no trace on the page.

I move my arm over to where Daniel should be sleeping. A wave of nausea rises from the black place, the great sucking hole, and I remember. It has been a week since he died.

I can't get enough air. I throw off the sheets, fumble for my glasses, switch on the light, and open the bedside dresser drawer, groping in the bottom where our printed emails have been kept for years. What if the dream was a portent? What if the words we wrote to each other have faded and the ink is no longer visible?

I reach under a book and a box of earrings, but the pages aren't there. I fall to my knees and look again. No luck.

Think, think. Where are they?

I rush upstairs to my study, where I yank open every drawer. *Ah, there they are.* I grab the stack of printed pages from the bookshelf and blink to clear my vision. "Family History, by John T. Saywell." My uncle's research about our ancestors.

I hurl it on the floor.

Downstairs, inside the red Chinese chest in the living room, I find a box filled with loose paper. Hope rising, I reach in. "Screenplay by Rob Paton." A friend's first draft of a feature film, which I'd once promised to read. The pages slip through my hands and cover the carpet like snowfall.

This is the thing they don't tell you about grief—the way things go missing, the way objects, big and small, disappear. A fog descends, panic sets in, the mind becomes a dysfunctional GPS. You tear around, desperate to find a piece of the person you've lost, knowing you can't afford to lose anything more.

I'm frantic now.

In the basement along one wall are built-in cupboards holding boxes of CDs, Christmas decorations, reel-to-reel tapes. I'm a madwoman, tearing every box open, flinging the contents everywhere.

I reach the last cupboard door and open it.

Sitting loosely stacked on top of a box of audiotapes, here they are. My most precious possession—our printed emails. The words of our story.

What are they doing abandoned in a damp corner of the basement? When did I put them here?

I'm on my knees, rocking back and forth, clutching them to my chest. More than a hundred pages filled with secrets and confessions, shared memories, and the reawakening of love. I run my palm over the top page, scan the first sentence.

I can't believe it, I had written.

Believe it at your own peril, Daniel had answered.

I am collapsed on the floor, surrounded by strewn boxes, the debris of the search. A shipwreck. Tears fill my ear canals and spill down my neck, soaking my hair.

Love. Lost.

Lost. Loss.

The words move around in my mind, like a word game. They have become interchangeable now.

Love. Loss.

Shards, jagged images from the past few months, keep washing up on the shore where I am marooned.

Lost.

After a time, a minute or maybe an hour, a word pairing comes to the rescue. *Lost and found.*

Our story is not erased, our emails are safe and sound. The ink has faded, but I can still make out the words that spelled a new beginning, when we found each other again.

Hourglass

A MAN LOOKS up from his drafting table and lets his eyes rest on the cherry blossoms outside his window. He is thinking of Japan. Every year in early spring the tree blooms, reminding him of his past. But this city in Utah is as far from the landscape of his childhood as one could imagine, and the delicate flowers of one tree will not bring it back. The Japanese have an expression for the emotion he is experiencing. *Mono no aware.* Everything is fleeting.

Maybe he will go for a short walk and shake off his nostalgic mood. Maybe he will get a whiff of something in the air and sense the undercurrent that is building, the seismic tremor about to shift his fault line.

He returns home and opens his computer. Types his name. Pushes Send.

A woman sits in her drafty attic study trying to meet a deadline. It's almost evening on a Saturday, and she needs to finish a narration script. She pushes a cassette into the slot, freezes on an image, noting the time code. *Think.* What words could explain the reason, the context, the precipitant history behind this haunting piece of film?

She pauses. Fingers hover over the keyboard.

Just out of frame, beyond this room, something is about to happen. She doesn't know this, but maybe she senses the liminal space. Cables under the ocean are thrumming, transporting trillions of words. Jettisoned out of the past, six words hurtle, headlong and unexpected, towards her.

There is a ping. A drop in the ocean of sound. The email has landed.

An early spring snow has begun to fall. She looks out the window at the white flakes spiralling through the darkening sky, unaware that the hourglass has been inverted and the past is coming back to reclaim her.

Classmates

THIS IS HOW I remember it.

Dusk was falling and my attic study was growing cold. I put the final touches on that script, then tidied the stack of videos and books strewn across my desk. Time to reclaim something of the weekend. Before I turned off the computer, I checked my inbox.

From: Classmates.com
Date: Saturday, April 7, 2002 4.51 PM
Subject: Shelley, you have a new Classmate

I bolted from my chair. Alley Cat unfurled and arched his back, and Dylan let out a strange, strangled meow.

"Oh my god oh my god."

I paced the floor, heart flapping like a wing. *Oh my god.*

I paced some more, then summoned the courage to sit back down and click open the message.

Daniel Peterson, Canadian Academy, Kobe, Japan.
Class of 73.

The power of his name—two simple words—made it hard to breathe.

Daniel Peterson. The boy I loved. At school he was known as Pete, short for Peterson.

Daniel. Pete. I hadn't seen or heard from him in almost thirty years.

I looked out the window to mark the moment. Snow was falling on rooftops. Lights were being switched on in the houses around me, windows becoming bright yellow boxes like in a child's drawing. The magic hour, cinematographers call it, when the sun disappears and leaves behind a perfect glow.

A memory began to form, with the opening chord progression of a song. *D–A–G–Em–Am7.*

Crosby, Stills & Nash is playing on the turntable. "Wooden Ships." A song about the universal language of a smile, the destruction of war, travelling through a foreign land.

It is 1972. The Vietnam War rages. I am a newcomer in Japan.

I look out the window and smile. Mist hangs low over Rokkō Mountain. From the dormitory window I see Pete in the distance, his gait unmistakable. He's probably headed up to the graveyard to have a smoke and play his harmonica. My eyes track him until he disappears into a blue haze. I don't know him yet; I always watch from afar.

I pick up the needle and replace it on the groove, wanting to hear the song again.

Now he is sitting, backlit by the window, on the opposite side of the classroom, slouched at his desk like a rebel, ready to bolt. I look down before he can catch me staring. I make a letter P on the page in my notebook and circle it twice.

The landscape of memory flowed like an old favourite song, reaching deep and pulling me in.

Daniel Peterson, Class of 73. I was staring at his name in my inbox. Could it really be so easy? Pete, whom I had wondered about for so many years, was just a click away? I pictured him as I had seen him last, walking away from me, tall and lanky, with a guitar case in his hand.

One false note had ruined our love song. I turned away, not waiting to see if he'd look back.

Now I was trying to remember. Was it a month, a week, an hour, or less before I was filled with regret? The letter I sent him came back slashed with red as if it had been stabbed—"person or address unknown."

I tried to find him. I mined our friends for information, but we were all graduates of an international school and scattered across the globe. The mail was slow, addresses changed, people moved on, and our grapevine eventually died. After a few years I set out for Japan to search for him, but fate intervened.

Daniel Peterson, Class of 73.

For years after we parted, I imagined meeting him again. I would create a scene, write a story in my head. I might enter a bar and discover his band was playing, or he'd appear in some dusty place I was filming in. I edited these fantasies over and over.

Scene: INTERIOR, MORNING. Pete is sitting in a seedy diner in a city that remains out of focus. He looks up in astonishment when I slide into the booth across from him.

Scene: A BEACH SOMEWHERE. The surf is pounding, the sun hot on my skin. A shadow falls over me and I hear his voice, saying, "Shelley?"

Over the years, at different times, I resumed the search again, most often during a rough patch when I found myself wondering *what if?* I had learned investigative skills from working on documentary films, but Daniel Peterson—of unknown location and unknown vocation—continued to elude me.

A new site called Classmates.com promised old school connections. I typed in my credit card number and added my name to the list of our graduating class, but Pete's name was missing. For the past six months the site had connected me to many old friends, but no one had heard from Pete.

Shelley, you have a new Classmate. How long had I been staring at the screen? I straightened my spine, planted my feet firmly on the floor, and began typing.

> Pete, it's Shelley. I can't believe it. Where have you been for 29 years? Write me.

I took a deep breath and pushed Send.

× × ×

"What's going on with you?" Kirsten and Susan asked, almost in unison. I'd been thinking that the wine tasted incredible—did I detect a hint of chocolate? I usually avoid wine; it gives me migraines. The aroma from the kitchen was making me ravenous.

"You are on planet Pluto," Susan said.

I'd been vaguely following their conversation about adopting a goat to support a family in Africa. "Of course I'll chip in on the goat," I said.

"We were discussing Susan's new sculpture!" Kirsten said, laughing. "We moved on from the goat fifteen minutes ago."

I laughed too, prickly heat rising in waves up my throat.

Kirsten shook her head in wonder when I finished the story. "I never knew you went to high school in Japan."

I had met Kirsten Scollie when I hired her as production manager on *Kim's Story: The Road from Vietnam*, my documentary about Kim Phuc, whose image had been captured in a searing photograph of the nine-year-old girl running down a road, naked, screaming, on fire from a napalm attack. Kim and I became close—I seem to make friends with most of the subjects of my films—and like all the other members of my crew, Kirsten became family. She and her romantic partner, Susan Fairbairn, were among my closest confidantes. But none of them knew this part of my past.

I said, "When Kim's village was bombed in 1972, I was headed for Japan and Pete was worried he could be drafted." Life suddenly seemed concentric.

"Wow," Kirsten said. "Do you think he'll write back?"

Logic said no; we had parted badly. But to reassure myself before coming to dinner, I'd searched for a photograph. It was one I had saved through a lifetime of moves from house-sits to shared apartments to a house of my own; I'd kept it tucked away during relationships and taken it out from time to time when I was alone, to remember when I was happiest.

I found the cardboard envelope filled with photographs from Japan on a bookshelf beside my journals. There we were: Pete and me at seventeen, on a train to Hiroshima. I'd gazed at our teenage selves—seeing in our faces the nakedness of love—and knew he could not have forgotten.

"Of course he'll write me back."

The conversation descended into a series of speculations from my two friends.

"He might be on his fifth wife by now."

"He could weigh seven hundred pounds."

"Maybe he's become a psycho. You never know."

"Maybe he's in prison."

A little drunk on wine and anticipation, I got home and raced upstairs to my study. I fired up the computer—and there he was in my inbox, just as I knew he would be. I took a deep breath and clicked Open.

Blue

AFTER I FOUND our printed emails in the corner of the basement, I put the pages inside a box covered with blue rice paper. It had been a gift one Christmas: a memory box, to hold our photos and letters. I place the box next to Daniel's blue chair.

I find other things and randomly add them to the box. Notes and cards and guitar picks, bits and pieces I stumble upon where they lie strewn about like emotional totems. Our house has become a minefield, threatening to blow me up every time I open a drawer. There might be a list for the hardware store in his handwriting, waiting like a tripwire, or a birthday card he wrote to me. I place them safely in the blue box. Safer for them and for me.

Mostly I shelter in the backyard, a private place hidden from my neighbour's view. I've started to haul slate to create a stone patio—an impulse—digging in the dirt and placing sand between each stone until sweat stings my eyes. I plant hellebores and ferns and a Japanese maple. Daniel had always wanted a garden like this, while I preferred roses and lavender. I will give him the garden he longed for. I work until my strength is gone, then go inside and stare at a wall.

This is your new life, I tell myself, so I measure time and set goals. How many hours do I have to stay awake? How many minutes have to drag across the desert of each day before night falls? How many hours of Netflix must I consume before I can take a sleeping pill and fall into oblivion?

Each morning I push Reset. Maybe I'll take a walk, actually leave the house.

The phone rings, but I let it go to voicemail. "Hi, it's Shelley and Daniel. Please leave us a message."

I should change the greeting. I go back to bed.

Rifling around for a bottle of Advil in the bedside drawer, I notice an indigo-coloured paper wallet of *mingei* design, so thin it almost disappears against the dark wood. Daniel gave me this wallet long ago, and I must have put it here for safekeeping. It's beautiful. A russet slip of paper, the size of a Post-it note, falls out. *MARRY ME*, it says, written in block letters in gold ink.

There's a sound like a bird smashing into a window. My water glass has shattered into splinters around me where I've collapsed on the floor.

Marry me. Daniel had already proposed in person. He'd used those same two words, not posed as a question. We joked about that—the certainty of it.

The note, which had accompanied an engagement ring, arrived a little later. It was inside a jewellery bag slung like a knapsack on the back of a stuffed toy monkey under the Christmas tree.

"So cute, Monkey Boy," I'd said, referring to Daniel's Chinese zodiac sign, and laughed.

He said, "Look inside."

I pulled out a ring. A blue sapphire, set in a lotus flower of gold filigree.

"Lotus is the symbol of female sexuality and rebirth," he told me.

In the years that followed, the monkey perched in different places around the house and the ring stayed on my finger, but the note had been tucked away. Forgotten, until it ambushed me.

Deadly, devastated, done.

It has been three weeks since he died. Today is my birthday. My friend Deborah Parks bravely shows up. We sit in the garden, sip coffee and cry. Deborah knows me almost as well as I know myself. She knows what this means, how deep the chasm is.

She believes that action is an antidote to most things. She's the person who persuaded me to take the leap from working for others to making our first documentary. In 1987, using a borrowed 16 mm Ari camera and donated camping gear, we spent a month in Egypt's eastern Sahara with Dr. Shahira Fawzy, an anthropologist. Shahira had been living among the Bishari, a nomadic people who did not appear on any census. They were once renowned as great warriors, but modern Egypt did not recognize their existence.

The Bishari did not speak Arabic, and as Shahira learned their unwritten language and listened to stories passed down through generations, she realized they spoke of ancient empires in the present tense. They showed her Roman cairns deep in the desert and asked her when Octavian's armies would return.

With Shahira, we stepped back in time, entering smoke-filled smugglers' dens, witnessing dervishes in ecstatic trances and intimate rituals in the women's camps. One night we filmed a warriors' dance—and watched in awe as a giant moon rose from the sand until its glowing orb filled the desert sky.

It was a grand adventure. We camped under the stars and traversed hundreds of miles across the sand. I got my first director's credit, and Deborah was awarded the Association of Canadian Cinematographers top prize, becoming the first woman ever to win it. Our film, *Shahira*, sold in twenty countries. We had put ourselves on the map in one go, and together we started a production company we called Bishari Films.

Deborah hands me a birthday gift, a ticket for the upcoming Georgia O'Keeffe and Alfred Stieglitz exhibition at the Art Gallery of Ontario. Deborah, who had once filmed at Ghost Ranch, where O'Keeffe lived and painted, is trying to find things that will bring me back to myself.

For a moment I am lifted, then a shadow descends. I am exhausted by her sweet efforts to mark my birthday and can't bear even the thought of the exhibit to come. Deborah was the one who got us to the Sahara, but I doubt she'll be able to get me out my front door.

A few weeks later we enter the cool gallery, joining a long line snaking through the exhibit. I move away from the crowd swarming around O'Keeffe's flowers, abandoning her seductive colours for the quieter side of the room, where Stieglitz's photographs hang in stark black-and-white. Most are intimate portraits of O'Keeffe.

The curators have quoted from his love letters. "How I wanted to photograph you—the hands—the mouth—& eyes, enveloped in black body—the touch of white—& the throat—" he wrote to her. His words of desire swim before my eyes. Across the room, O'Keeffe's flowers stare back, defiant with beauty and life. How did she go on after Stieglitz died?

"I need to leave," I whisper to Deborah. She nods and drives me home. The traffic on Dundas Street is snarled. A siren wails. The gallery is only a few blocks from Princess Margaret, the hospital where Daniel was treated.

My bare legs seem ghostly in the bathroom light. They feel disconnected from me. So do the hands that turn on the bathwater. A thought breaks through: one person's grief is infinitesimal, a mere drop in an ocean of suffering that makes up the human condition. I should know; I've been a filmmaker of sorrow. But before I lost Daniel, I never understood its weight and scope.

I let the hot water run until the bath is almost scalding, in the Japanese way, then climb in. Wince, shudder, release. I reach into memory to feel his touch on me.

Today is overcast and cool, a respite from the heat. I am sitting in his blue chair, the one he loved because it is the colour of Japanese indigo, with the memory box at my feet. I take out the emails and put them in my lap, caressing them like a lover.

Dear Shelley . . .

My eyes cloud. I remember reading Daniel's words for the first time, in the spring of 2002. Even then I was remembering. Japan when we were seventeen. I remember remembering.

My heart had swelled like an ocean wave, cresting with each sentence. Now I fear the undertow. What if I've remembered things badly? What if his words take on a different meaning, now that there is no possibility of my asking him what he meant?

Date: April 7, 2002 8:30 PM
Subject: BELIEVE IT; AT YOUR OWN PERIL

Dear Shelley,
I won't even try to count the years; not enough fingers even by half . . . but what a positively delightful surprise to hear from you. I really don't know where to start, but as in most cases, the beginning

> would seem to be the place; the following is the definitive "in his own write" version of the brief bio.

When I first read those words, it was past one in the morning. My attic study was illuminated only by the computer screen. I could feel my blood pulsing. I was about to learn where he had been and who he had become; his words would solve a ten-thousand-day-old mystery.

> I dropped out of university after a year plus change and went back to Japan. After a few months I got a letter from a friend asking me to come to the US and start a band. I spent about ten years in Nashville, working with various groups doing road and studio work . . .

Pete, the teenage boy I had known, had been headed to Ann Arbor University to study classical Chinese. Instead, he had become a professional musician in Nashville! My eyes raced and skipped through his sentences like a pebble over water, scanning for the significant.

Married . . . disillusioned . . . a stranger in the States, missed Japan terribly . . .

And then the word I was searching for.

Divorced. Without a mate for the past several years.

I printed the email and took it to bed and read it over and over.

× × ×

In Daniel's chair, in our living room, I read those words again. He had written that he didn't go by the name Pete anymore. He signed it *Daniel/Pete.*

Memory folds into itself, encasing two chapters of my life. Pete, who I knew in Japan, and Daniel, who came after.

I place the emails back in their blue box, my heart too full to read more today. In need of an old friend, one I knew even before him, I put on Joni Mitchell's *Blue.* I shut my eyes, thinking about the way time spins and circles, slows down, then races past, finally running out like sand in an hourglass.

Hey, Blue . . .

Everyone calls me Shell, for Shelley. Like Joni's lullaby, whear a sigh from this empty shell that only memory can fill.

Pete and I are sitting on the beach where two rivers join the sea. Golden glow, sea salt air. He smiles. Freeze the frame. Fade to blue.

Things We Remember

DANIEL PROMISED HE would never leave me again, but after we had flown back to Toronto, received the diagnosis, and spent ten traumatic months in and out of hospitals, he was gone.

Somewhere along the way I've lost all notion of time. I know from the calendar that it's been six weeks since he died. My mind flickers from one scene to another, disoriented and jumbled, until time collapses and then means nothing at all.

"How did you meet?" The young woman doctor with golden hair who looked like an angel asked us. We were in the radiation waiting room at Princess Margaret Cancer Centre, filling out forms.

I'd flown home after seventy-two hours in Italy and met Daniel's flight from D.C. We'd gone from the airport straight to Emergency, where we learned that Daniel had stage IV small-cell lung cancer—the quick one, the worst one. His disease came accompanied by weight gain, a condition called Cushing's syndrome, which can be brought on by tumours. This was a trickster, because one of the telltale symptoms of cancer is usually weight loss. Over the past year, Daniel had not understood why he kept gaining weight, despite daily workouts, long hours of physical labour, and a healthy vegetarian diet. The weight distressed him, and he had begun to draw away from our physical connection.

"You still look sexy," I'd say, wanting to seduce him.

He'd sigh with exhaustion, but before rolling over to sleep, he'd kiss me goodnight and tell me not to worry. "I will always be your lover."

I believed him. After his next deadline, after my next film, we would rest, reignite and rediscover the desire that had lasted through decades of separation and almost fourteen years back together. But deep down I always feared our happiness was too great, that it might tempt the gods.

I knew that life was precarious. Four years earlier, Daniel had survived a massive heart attack. It was a terrifying, unexpected wake-up call, after which we had thanked our lucky stars and clung even closer to one another. He quit smoking, something he had tried and failed at so often before. But it was already too late. The recent weight gain and lethargy concealed a sneaky, deadly cancer that had spread, with breathtaking speed, from a tumour in his lung into his bloodstream and then lodged in his cervical spine. There it created lesions that, when finally discovered, made his doctors fear he might become a paraplegic.

The oncologist prepared us for the effects of radiation, a palliative treatment to reduce the excruciating pain. "We'll do an initial round, but it might make it worse for a while. Radiation causes swelling."

We were grasping at straws, the initial shock of the diagnosis now supplanted by a single goal: to release him from pain. This was a new world of agony and fear.

The pretty young doctor was trying to distract us. "You met in Japan?"

"High-school sweethearts," Daniel said, squeezing my hand.

"Yes," I added, smiling. "And we fell in love twice."

× × ×

Dear Daniel,

It feels strange to call you Daniel, but after (gasp) 29 years why not? To me you will always be Pete.

My Story: I finished university without a clue what I wanted, and literally fell into my career. I am a documentary filmmaker. It seems to satisfy my desire to be creative and my addiction to news and world events. I've been lucky to be able to make films on subjects I care about. The latest is about war-affected children in Chechnya, Sierra Leone, and the Middle East.

I was married once, ages ago, and I'm now in a relationship with a former colleague, but we don't live together.

I know what you mean about this feeling unreal. It's odd to describe one's life in a truncated way to someone you once knew well but don't know anymore.

I have this great picture of us on a train. You look very laid back, with long hair and an earring. I'm wearing a big grin. It's nice to have such good memories.

The photograph was a coded invitation. I knew if he remembered the day it was taken, he would write to me again.

Becoming

A TEENAGE GIRL, thin, just shy of gangly, with a shag haircut and a mouth a little large for her face, boards a Greyhound bus for Massachusetts. She's carrying a duffel bag and a guitar. In the photo you don't see fear, but it's there if you look closely. She has volunteered to spend her summer living and working with the American Friends Service Committee, founded by the Quakers.

She is not yet sixteen. Somehow, she persuaded her parents to let her go. What does a Toronto girl know of America's inner cities, racism, civil protest, bearing witness? She tells herself she will be okay.

She joins a commune of fourteen volunteers, all American, all older than she is, housed in a derelict building on the shore of the Atlantic in New Bedford, Massachusetts. There are children of immigrants from Cape Verde, Africa, playing in the spray of a fire hydrant. Police cruisers slow down so the cops can taunt her African-American coworkers. There are shootings on the street. This is the summer she will smoke her first joint, taste her first French kiss, learn about Malcolm X. Walking on the beach at night listening to Jim Morrison, she thinks about new horizons, the expanded scope of her life. She will come back to Toronto with a feeling that her eyes are now open.

A teenage boy skulks off, wanting to be alone. He takes the wooded paths up Black Mountain, North Carolina, hiking as far as he can get from the gathering of evangelicals his missionary parents have brought him to. He's grown his hair long and pierced one ear. He looks older than fifteen.

His parents are on furlough from their mission in Shikoku, Japan. He didn't want to come back to the States with them, just like the last time, when he was very young and refused to speak anything but Japanese.

But America has its hooks in him too. The music, mostly. He's bought a stack of albums to take back to Japan, new releases that haven't made it there: *Sticky Fingers*, *Who's Next*, *Led Zeppelin IV*, *Fragile* by Yes. He is stirred by something he can't put his finger on; perhaps it's just that no one stares at him here and he can be invisible. The Blue Ridge Mountains, resting place of his ancestors, hold a part of him too.

It's the beginning of dislocation, an internal dialogue. *Who am I? Where is home?*

What Lies Ahead

ONE DAY AFTER Daniel's shattering diagnosis, unable to process what was happening, I went to see the hospital psychiatrist.

"I have no hope," I told her.

"You have hope. It's just different now. You hope for different things."

I thought about that and realized she was right. I did have hope. Every day I hoped I could comfort him, help relieve his pain, make him smile, cook something he could swallow.

"But I can't see what lies ahead," I said in a small voice. "I can't make a decision."

"Assess as you go," she said.

I seized on this notion like a lifeline. *Assess as you go* was a tool precisely suited to both a medical situation and a crisis of the heart, and I needed all the tools I could get.

"Be compassionate and forgive, especially yourself," she added.

I left her office wondering if I would ever be able to forgive Daniel for getting sick and erasing our future. Could I forgive myself for the years we had spent apart?

Assess as you go. She was right; it was the way to move forward, and it was the kind of thinking that would get me through the hours and days and weeks ahead. Focusing on the here and now, triaging Daniel's changing needs, would help me hide the grief that was already lodged inside me.

But there was a flaw in this approach: I didn't want to move ahead. All I wanted was to go back and start over.

× × ×

Summer, 1972. From the outlook of the Forbidden City, Beijing stretches as far as the horizon. The brown-grey air is smoky from a million charcoal cooking fires and filled with sand that has blown in from the Gobi Desert. Everything is bleak, dusted in grit. Even the grass has been plucked out of the ground, leaving the earth bald and dry and stirring loose with each hot gust of wind. This is the result of the latest decree: "Comrades! Grass must be eliminated to prevent insect infestation." On the wide boulevards below, the only colour to be seen is the vivid red of propaganda posters, hanging like slash marks from windows and rooftops.

I enter the palace, trailing my family. The chambers and corridors hold priceless treasures gathering dust: bronzes and jade carvings, exquisite and rare, neglected and shrouded in silence. Chinese citizens aren't allowed inside these walls.

There are no tourists. We are the privileged few, a select group of foreign diplomats and their families recently let into the country.

The Forbidden City is so vast that one wrong turn will get you lost. The halls seem to echo with the ghosts of emperors and eunuchs, the shuffle of lily feet, the sweep of silk robes. Falling into a trancelike state, I imagine the past coming to life, like a scene in *Dream of the Red Chamber.*

I have just turned seventeen. In another world, maxi dresses and miniskirts reign, protests against the war in Vietnam rage, Watergate makes the news, and Neil Young has released *Heart of Gold*. I'd planned to volunteer with the Quakers again this summer, feeding my hunger for independence. Instead I'm in Beijing with my family, where my father has just been appointed First Secretary at the Canadian embassy.

Beyond the palace walls, a grim, monolithic China has spent the past twenty years cut off from the world. Its inner workings have been a mystery for longer than I've been alive. This is the first crack in the armour, the first sliver of a view. On the streets, girls my age recite slogans from Mao Zedong's *Little Red Book*, wearing their hair in plaits or unflattering bowl cuts, without jewellery or makeup to adorn their beautiful faces. Drab green or grey uniforms complete the picture of conformity. Anonymity means safety.

This goes against everything I've learned in life so far. Last summer I was taught by the Quakers to bear witness, and by my fellow volunteers that to fight for social justice you need to stand up, stand out, be heard. Not here.

In the streets of Beijing, people crane their necks and stare openly. On the way here we were surrounded by a big crowd.

"They tried to touch my hair," says Jim. My brother has just turned thirteen and is letting his blond hair grow long.

"Why does everyone wear the same clothes?" asks Trish, our ten-year-old sister.

Our father tells us China was an experiment where everyone is supposed to be equal, but things have gone awry. That the country is opening and emerging after six dark years of the Cultural Revolution. This is his first time inside China, a professional coup for an academic who teaches modern Chinese political history. He was asked by our government to take the post because he is valuable as a "China watcher"—someone who speaks the language, can analyze signs from the Politburo and speculate on the significance of public appearances by members of Mao's inner circle and the fate of those no longer visible. For the first time since 1949, when diplomatic relations were severed, Western embassies are reopening in China.

Of course, we see nothing of the true cost or destructiveness of Mao's ongoing campaigns—the Red Guard attacks on "bourgeois elements," the persecution of intellectuals, the untold numbers of people who were taken to the countryside for re-education, tortured, murdered, or have committed suicide.

We live in a bubble at the Min Zhu Hotel, across from Tiananmen Square, waiting to move into an apartment in a complex under construction for foreigners. When the afternoons are hot, we go for a dip in the embassy pool. Two separate worlds, divided by a gate.

After a month in Beijing, I'm still not accustomed to the strange duality. My family and I live cloistered in luxury while outside there is toil and poverty, fear and distrust of us and of each other, but also national pride. Riding our bikes into the *hutongs*—warrens of narrow streets lined with traditional courtyard homes that are now crowded with shanties—we pass workers who pedal impossible loads on their bicycles, women cooking over open fires, and small children squatting to relieve themselves in the streets. The air is infused with the smells of iron, garlic and sweat. In communist China the individual is deemed to be part of a great machine, working for the collective good. Such a contrast to the pursuit of individualism I have been raised to believe in.

Summer flies by in a whirlwind of outings: picnics at the Ming tombs, day trips to villages that time seems to have abandoned, visits to communes and hospitals, a week at the seaside in Beidaihe, and a trip to Tianjin, on the edge of the Bohai Sea, where we shop in a store just for foreigners and buy embroidered silk robes and hair clips with peacock feathers that might have adorned a concubine. We see a number of elderly Caucasians wander into a tea shop that still makes Hungarian pastries; they are likely refugees from one of Europe's wars or revolutions, here to take tea as though unaware the world has moved on. *Every person has a story to tell*, I think. I develop a crush on a French cameraman who's on assignment, covering Asia from his base in Hong Kong.

We meet and have a conversation, one day when I'm on my own. I romanticize his line of work. As he leaves, he slips me his card with a phone number.

There's so much to experience here, but as summer draws to a close, I'm ready to claim a little independence and excited to be going away to school. My younger brother and sister will stay in Beijing and study by correspondence, but I am entering my senior year of high school. Before we left Toronto I had been given a choice: I could stay in Canada or go to boarding school anywhere in the world, courtesy of the Canadian government. My girlfriends swooned as I flipped through brochures from schools in the Swiss Alps, but I chose one in Kobe, Japan. I wanted to stay in Asia. And the school called to me with its surprising name: Canadian Academy.

"When you arrive, please cable the embassy to let us know you got there," my dad says, hugging me. My mom makes a joke and tries not to cry. My brother hands me a gift, a ring he chose himself and saved up to buy me. My sister throws her arms round my waist. It's hard to say goodbye.

China is so isolated from the Western world that there are no direct flights to anywhere outside the communist bloc. The journey to Japan will take several days. Somehow that thought makes the distance that will lie between me and my family seem even greater.

In the airport lounge I distract myself with imaginings about the people around me. There's the diplomatic courier, a man who takes packages in and out for the embassy, and a secretary going on furlough. *Maybe they are having an affair.* There's a Persian couple from the newly established Embassy of Iran. She is very beautiful. *Maybe they are members of the Pahlavi royal family.* Next to them is a Japanese man—*he might be negotiating diplomatic ties between their countries.* As my father has often reminded me, we are among the very few foreigners who've been allowed in and out of China since 1949. I know we are sharing a unique moment in time, but time seems to hang.

We all joke about the usual delays. Finally we are boarding the Soviet-built propeller plane, entering a cabin crowded with passengers carrying cages of livestock.

The plane makes a steep ascent through the brown Beijing skies. "Steady, girl." The diplomatic courier smiles at me. "You look a little green." He's right; I barely manage to push down a wave of nausea.

In Guangzhou, all foreign travellers are escorted to Min Tzu Fan Dian, the People's Hotel. The night is long and sleepless. Watching the ceiling fan, drifting in and out, my thoughts turn from what it might be like where I'm going to thinking about where I've been.

In the morning, a bus and then a train take us on a two-hour journey to the border. When the train slows and pulls up to the platform at the Lo Wu Border Processing Centre, we hand over our passports and are shown into a colonial-style building, down a hall and into a large reception room with tables set for lunch. We are offered Guangdong *mian*, Cantonese noodles. Our hosts are gracious, but no one is smiling.

Hours go by. For something to do, I pocket a package of the complimentary cigarettes that line every ashtray, even though I don't smoke; accept a cup of steaming hot water served in lieu of tea; find one of the overstuffed white chairs and sit down to wait. I think about the friends I've left in Toronto. I think about the American friends I made in New Bedford, Massachusetts, last summer. I think of my family in Beijing. Simultaneous separate worlds, all a part of me.

Eventually visas are stamped, passports are returned and we are free to leave. We walk past People's Liberation Army soldiers carrying SKS rifles and into no man's land, then across a bridge towards a unit of Gurkhas manning a checkpoint flying the Union Jack.

Onboard the Kowloon-Canton Railway train, our small group, bonded by spending two days together, begins to cheer. Conversations flow, time speeds up, and in two short hours we are in Hong Kong.

I lived here at thirteen when my dad was on a sabbatical. I was a student at the British Island School. I know the streets and sounds and smells; this feels like a homecoming.

To celebrate my status as a newly independent person, as soon as I check into my room in a posh hotel in the Ocean Terminal, I take the pack of Chinese cigarettes from my purse and light my first cigarette. The next day I take the Star Ferry to our old neighbourhood, remembering how I'd once yearned to be older, and feeling almost grown. Outside the building on McDonald Road where we had rented an apartment, the same milk, fruit and bread ladies sell their wares on the sidewalk. Four years have passed, and my viewpoint is from a higher angle, but everything evokes a form of déjà vu.

Spending the money I had been given for school supplies, I buy knockoff record albums from vendors in the alleys, a Mary Quant lipstick at the Lane Crawford department store, and a minidress to wear to dinner with the dashing French cameraman I'd met in Beijing. It's sort of a date—my first. Things go well until I tell him my age and he chokes on his martini. Then everything shifts. He confides his fears: he will soon leave on assignment to Vietnam. I confess mine: going to a new school in a new country. He escorts me back to my hotel after dinner and takes me to the airport the next day.

Onboard the JAL flight bound for Osaka, everything finally sinks in. There is no telephone connection with mainland China. Mail from my family will be sporadic, delivered in diplomatic pouches by human couriers. I'm heading to a place where I don't know a soul. A boarding school. I suddenly feel like a child. After the glowing lights of Hong Kong recede, all I can see is the small red wing light flashing in the dark.

× × ×

Dear Daniel,

Thank you for writing to me. I was scared last night after I sent my email that it would be the end of the chain; that after I'd written my reply, you wouldn't write back.

I feel as though we are sharing a diary, and it's taking me to a place I want to be in. If you are inclined, please keep going as much or little as you like. If not, I understand. It's hard to be in the throes of memory, it casts a different light.

Dear Shelley,
I've never had the opportunity to connect with someone from my past, much less someone I was close to. This recent correspondence with you is exhilarating, disorienting, revealing and bewildering. I cherish it and it is something I want to continue.

A New Life

IT HAS BEEN two months since Daniel died.

A producer calls to talk about a new documentary celebrating Margaret Atwood. Would I direct? Like a ghostly image on a photographic plate, I feel a whisper of my old self. I pull a beloved volume of Atwood's poetry from my bookshelf and sit down to read, but the words won't settle on the page.

I meet him and his co-producer for lunch on the patio of a fancy club on Bloor Street. Around us, people wear expensive linen and sip white wine. "Work will help you climb out of grief," he says. His wife died of breast cancer years ago, and work was what kept him going.

The light is blinding on the patio, and I wonder if it's rude to keep my sunglasses on. My dress feels damp, my chest feels heavy. I nod and try to listen. My right ear throbs, my head pounds.

"You are perfect for this," they are saying. "Graeme

Gibson, Margaret's husband, has dementia. You need to talk to him before his memories are gone."

I try to imagine this, but it is too much to fathom. I don't want to make a film. I want to go home and lie down.

In the safety of my house, my face muscles release, aching from the effort of trying to look normal. Here I can stop pretending and return to the void. My new life.

People have been leaving packages on my porch. Friends and neighbours have been so incredibly kind. Almost every day I've found something there: homemade meals, wine, flowers, bath salts, essential oils, coffee and chocolates. Yesterday a friend left Joan Didion's *The Year of Magical Thinking.* I'd read it years ago, moved by its tragic beauty and power, but this time I read it for clues. How does anyone survive this? I stumble upon a passage that explains my mystery earache, about how survivors "clogged their sinuses with unshed tears and ended up in otolaryngologists' offices with obscure ear infections. They lost concentration."

After taking two courses of antibiotics for my throbbing inflamed right ear with no effect, I have an appointment at the eye, ear and throat clinic of Mount Sinai Hospital.

The specialist examines me. "You do not have an ear infection."

I look at him blankly. Two doctors have already looked at my ear and told me I do.

"You have been clenching your jaw, which is what's causing the throbbing in your ear."

I do a mental body scan. There is tension in my temples, cheekbones, jaw, neck and shoulders; my mid and lower back are also aching.

I call Xiaolan, our doctor of traditional Chinese medicine. She takes me into a small room that smells of camphor and herbs, sits across a small table from me and holds my wrists.

"You are too hot," she says, looking closely at my pupils. "You are not sleeping." She asks after Daniel, whom she has treated in the past.

"Daniel died."

"I didn't know. I'm so sorry." She sighs, still holding my wrists, and shakes her head. "Grief." She tells me to lie down and puts acupuncture needles in my back. I flinch.

"You still have fear," she says.

The first line in C.S. Lewis's *A Grief Observed* is about fear. He wrote that he had never understood that grief could feel so much like fear. My body knows this to be true: my heart is constantly racing. I wonder what frightens me so much, since the worst thing has already happened. Then it dawns on me. The worst thing is not that Daniel died. The worst is the nothingness. I expected to hear his voice guiding me, telling me it would be okay. There is only silence.

Xiaolan's hands are cool on my forehead. "Lie here for a while," she says, and leaves the room. The needles do their work.

I'm drifting. The darkness behind my eyelids becomes night and my tears become rain.

× × ×

I can't see a thing. The cascading rivulets of water on the windshield blur highway signs, then streetlights, until they become slashes of red, blue and white. It's after ten at night, pitch dark, and the taxi is speeding in the driving rain along the freeway from Osaka Airport to Kobe. The driver makes a sudden turn and navigates a steep incline up a mountain road, windshield wipers working furiously. I hold my breath, praying the car will make it to the top. When we reach the ridge, he pulls up to a building and brakes. The headlights illuminate a sign that says "Canadian Academy, Girls' Dorm" in English, with Japanese characters underneath.

I hold open my wallet to let him pull out what he needs. I say, "*Dōmo arigatō.*" Thank you. It's the only Japanese I know. We get out and he opens the trunk and hands me my suitcase. Within seconds we are completely drenched.

After pulling my bag inside the double glass doors, I'm in a vestibule with a small sign that says *genkan* and wooden shelves lined with shoes. I take off my soaking sneakers, mop my hair with the back of my sleeve, and enter the main room. There is a pay phone, a bulletin board and some worn sofas and chairs. No one is around.

Giggles. I look up. A group of girls are leaning over the railing on the second floor, staring down at me.

"We've been expecting you for hours," a male voice says. I whirl around and see a man approaching from his apartment across the hall. He looks impossibly old.

"I'm sorry. I was held up at immigration in Osaka." In the hubbub of moving from Canada to China, some things, including my student visa, had been overlooked. The Japanese customs officials kept me in a room at the airport for hours, until they could reach someone at the Canadian embassy in Tokyo on a Sunday night. I'm tired and very wet.

"Well, good thing you've arrived—we lock the door in a few minutes. I'm Mr. Williams. My wife and I are your dorm parents."

He leads me up the stairs, now abandoned, to a room on the second floor. It's an indeterminate shade of dusty pink or grey and the floor is brown linoleum.

"This is your roommate, Celia." A girl with long blonde hair is lying on one of the beds. She looks up from her book and her blue eyes narrow, sizing me up. I must look like a drowned rat. Mr. Williams asks Celia to help me get settled and makes his retreat.

There's a large wooden crate in front of the unclaimed bed, marked "Diplomatic Immunity."

"Got a body in there?" Celia asks, clearly prepared to hate me.

"Just drugs," I joke. I toss my handbag on the empty bed, and out tumbles lip gloss and comb, chewing gum, passport and the Xinhua cigarettes I pocketed at the Chinese border.

There's a sharp rap on the door. Celia aims her pillow at me, and it lands on my bed just as Mrs. Williams enters. Wearing a tight smile, she looks like a faded Norman Rockwell painting, her watery eyes peering at me over wire-rimmed glasses. She welcomes me with a recitation of rules.

"Lights out soon," she says, and closes the door behind her.

"That was a close call."

"Huh?"

"Those weird-looking cigarettes on your bed. Are you crazy? We aren't allowed to smoke here." Celia springs up and lifts the pillow covering them.

"I thought you were aiming at me!"

She breaks into an infectious laugh that I can't help catching. Soon we are practically in hysterics.

"If it stops raining, we can sneak out and have a smoke before bed," she says.

It's the beginning of a beautiful friendship.

× × ×

Dear Shelley,

It is not at all my intention to overwhelm the moment, but after writing you in what can only be described as a sublimely unguarded state of mind and heart, I must tell you that I was inundated by memories of "those times" all day long, to the point that I had to stop working and just let the thoughts and images take their course. There is a particular set of memories I want to share with you.

He wrote about the trip when our photograph was taken. He remembered everything.

Dear Daniel,

I must have reread your letter 10 times before falling asleep last night, and I too have been thrown into a dreamlike state. Some of the memories are so strong I can almost smell, hear, touch them. I remember filters of sunlight on tatami, remember the shoji screen opening to the sea, and I remember you in your vintage army jacket sitting, looking out at the view, drinking tea. I hadn't forgotten, but it all came back so vividly.

It's Only Love

MONDAY MORNING. I woke early and threw off the covers, rushed upstairs to my computer and clicked the mail icon. There was his name in my inbox, time-stamped in the American west and sent in the middle of the night.

I drank in every word with my coffee. Our email exchange was only three days old but already brimming with questions, comments, opinions, details and a few long-awaited answers. It was as though we had unleashed a magic clock that moved backwards, making me feel younger by the moment.

I threw on my jacket and began walking to work, selecting Sheryl Crow on my iPod. I was too hyper to wait for the streetcar, too impatient to stand still at the crosswalk. The last patches of snow were melting in the spring sunshine, the city was coming alive. I pounded the pavement, the rhythm of the music pacing my footfalls, until the lyrics of "It's Only Love" stopped me in my tracks.

Sheryl was singing about meeting her match again, in a blaze of love that melted ice. I felt a flush of heat rise from my toes to the top of my head. I had not seen Pete in almost three decades. Who knew if chemistry lasted?

The song would become my mantra. If only love would come round again, all the choices I'd made in my life, all the mistakes, could be seen as destined. Everything would have been worth the ride, if I was headed back to Pete.

In the edit room, Deborah Palloway, my film editor, looked up quizzically. "Shell, what's going on?"

She and I had worked together for more than ten years and had been friends for even longer. I had my head down, digging into my bag for my notebook and pen, ready to plunge into work, but there was no escaping her scrutiny.

Deb had seen me through a failed marriage and had been there for me throughout the complicated relationship I was now involved in, with an older man, the venerable journalist and film producer Michael Maclear. Michael had made his name covering the Vietnam War from North Vietnam. He was the sole Western journalist at the funeral of Ho Chi Minh, and he had reported from the ground on the Christmas bombing of Hanoi. He'd given me my first break, hiring me as a researcher on his series *Vietnam: The Ten Thousand Day War.* I was twenty-three when we met; in my thirties we began an affair. He was a brilliant, sexy and funny man, but he was also a depressive, twenty-six years my senior and married. Our relationship was marred by guilt. Even after he moved out and was legally separated from his wife, he refused to "go public" or live with me.

Whenever I tried to end it, he clung to me, possessive, jealous and moody. For years I had been settling for less than I wanted out of life, throwing my passion instead into the stories I told in film.

Deb was one of the friends to whom I'd confessed it all, almost from the beginning. We knew each other's parents and pets. We snuck off to get high at parties and film festivals. Together we celebrated buying our first homes and other milestones. As a reward, when we reached "picture lock" on a film, we would go to New York to do the narration recording at Todd AO Studios and then visit art galleries, shop in Soho and have a celebratory dinner. The last time we were there, seven months earlier, we'd recorded Christopher Plummer narrating *A Child's Century of War* and had ended the evening at the News and Documentary Emmys, where I stood onstage holding the glimmering prize for our film *Crimes of Honour.* It was five days before 9/11.

Since then, the world had changed. Since I'd said goodbye to Deb on Friday, I had changed too.

Like the brilliant editor she was, Deb didn't miss much. "You look different."

It had been exactly forty-eight hours since that first email exchange with Daniel/Pete. I could scarcely eat, my body a mass of nerve endings that seemed to be rewiring.

I opened the window overlooking Spadina Avenue and inhaled the scent of early spring. The shouts of children in a nearby schoolyard rose from the street. A train whistled in the distance. Had those sounds and smells been there before?

"What happened?" she asked.

I turned and met her eye. "I woke up."

Monday morning, Canadian Academy, thirty years earlier.

An alarm ringing somewhere is trying to penetrate a dream. It takes me a moment. One eye opens, then shuts again as reality sinks in. I'm in a room in the girls' dorm. I pull the pillow over my head to muffle the sounds of forty girls scurrying down the hall. Need more sleep.

My roommate's voice. "Hurry up, you'll miss breakfast."

Moan.

I get in line to brush my teeth in the communal bathroom. *God.*

Throw on jeans and stumble outside, rubbing sleep from my eyes, and trail Celia into the dark cafeteria, which smells of burning grease. The room is a mess of long tables with dirty trays and empty chairs.

"We're late."

I grab a plastic mug, fill it with coffee. Ah, yes, coffee will save me. It's my addiction; I've loved the taste ever since the age of four, when my parents' Hungarian Jewish landlady gave me a sip of steaming brew with its enticing aroma when I snuck downstairs to her kitchen.

I take a sip. A lukewarm liquid washes down my throat in a wave of disappointment. I try a bite of the lumpy oatmeal and push the bowl away.

Celia grabs two packets of cookies and hands one to me. "Breakfast."

We head out past the stream of day students starting to arrive, past Gloucester House, the original principal's residence, which is now the boys' dorm. Someone shouts to Celia and she waves up at the window, grabbing my arm to make me move faster. Back in our dorm room, there's just enough time for a shower and to pull a comb through my hair.

"I gotta go," Celia says, and grabs her books. She laughs. "Tomorrow you'd better get up when the alarm goes off."

It's my first moment alone.

Our bedroom window faces the mountain rising to the west. The walls need paint; they are gouged and marked. There are two single beds, one shared bookcase, and two wooden desks. A metal bar props up the lid of my desk, revealing a mirror underneath. I catch a glimpse. Brown eyes, freckled nose, and a shag cut finally growing out.

I look through the clothes I've dumped on the bed and consider first impressions. I choose a favourite sundress that once belonged to my great-aunt Helen, a woman with a tragic story. During the Depression, Helen had left her family's farm in Millbrook, Ontario, to work in Buffalo, New York. She got a job as a nurse. She was murdered, her body found in the apartment she rented. Rumours were rife but the crime was never solved. Maybe the murderer had been a lover, or a jealous wife. Or maybe it was random.

Because I loved vintage clothes, my grandmother had given me the contents of her sister-in-law's trunk a few months before we left for Beijing: jackets with padded shoulders and men's-style trousers, velvet evening coats and gowns—the clothes of a spirited young woman seeking glamour and independence. They fitted me perfectly.

Adjusting the straps of the faded blue and white sundress, I pull my shoulders back and down, seeking courage for my first day, and head for the headmaster's office.

Principal Chudler greets me warmly. "Welcome. You are our first student from Beijing!" He leaves the room to cable my father, confirming that I've arrived.

I look out his window. The rain clouds have lifted and the fog is burning off, revealing a spectacular setting. The school is nestled on a ridge of Nagamine Mountain, part of the Rokkō range, overlooking Kobe's harbour.

Before I head to class, I pick up a brochure from a stack on his desk and look through it. *Canadian Academy was founded by Canadian Methodists in 1913, with 16 students. It was used as an internment camp in the Second World War, bombed and burned almost to the ground. Of the original buildings only Gloucester House and the academic building remain.*

Everyone, including Principal Chudler, calls the school "CA." It's become an international school and I am one of only two actual Canadians.

I find my classroom and take a seat next to the window. *Click.* Looking up over my glasses I notice a Japanese boy, his bangs in his eyes, pointing a Nikon at me. *Click.* I frown, because I hate being caught in my glasses. I need them to see the blackboard, but the rest of the time they stay in my bag.

"That's Mark. Don't let him bother you; he's the school photographer." A girl wearing an ankle-length batik skirt and a straw hat sits down next to me. She looks decidedly cool—wide-eyed, with golden-brown hair falling almost to her waist—a sort of gamine hippie.

She pulls out her notebook and tells me, "I decided to sit next to the most interesting-looking person in the room. Love the dress. My name is Alexandra, but everyone calls me Zazie."

We smile in mutual admiration. I think I'm going to like this place.

After classes end for the day, I go for a walk, wanting to get my bearings. Passing the cafeteria building and pottery studio and gymnasium, I cross a wide lawn that stretches to the edge of the ridge, which is reinforced by giant boulders. I stare down at the harbour far below, which is shaped like a horizontal peace sign, sparkling in the light.

A white bird soars overhead. The late afternoon sun casts everything in silhouette.

I don't see him at first. Then something draws my eye—perhaps he moves.

The main academic building, a Tudor-style structure, is nestled against the mountain, flanked by giant fir trees. He is sitting on the balustrade of the wide steps at its entrance. I squint into the sunlight. Long brown hair hangs to his shoulders. There's the glint of an earring. One of his legs is bent at the knee, a cowboy boot casually resting on the stone. He looks up and smiles.

I am blinded. His from this moment on.

A shadow falls on my path, cast by a girl walking towards him. I realize that his smile is not for me. She sits down next to him, his arms circle her waist and he pulls her closer. I do not move, watching as they kiss.

In the sunlight of this September day, everything else falls away. There is only one thought, only one sensation.

I want to be that girl.

Ink Stain

SOON AFTER DANIEL got home from the hospital, a couple of weeks after his diagnosis, Zazie called, waking me up. I looked at the clock—it felt later, but it was just before midnight.

I stumbled in the dark to grab the phone, hoping the sleeping pill he'd taken would allow Daniel to sleep through the sound.

"Hello?"

"Shell, it's Za." She giggled, then asked, "Did I wake you?"

She often called as her whirlwind New York life was winding down for the night. She was curator of contemporary Asian art at the Guggenheim Museum, always busy, travelling, writing books, attending events or creating groundbreaking shows.

"Hi, Za," I whispered, groping my way downstairs in the dark.

"You sound strange," she said.

"Daniel is sleeping, so I'm speaking softly."

"Is everything okay?"

Oh god, here it was. The conversation I was not ready for.

"I . . . no . . . Daniel is sick . . ."

"Shelley . . . ?"

"Lung cancer, stage IV."

"No."

My words were spilling out now, blunt, jagged, distant, as though coming from someone else. "Italy . . . holiday . . . didn't realize . . . so much pain . . . might have a few years."

I was making a mess of the telling, like an overturned inkwell spreading its dark stain. We hadn't told people yet, because saying it out loud would make it real. This first attempt was not going well.

I was also fighting the effects of the sleeping pill I'd taken, and searching the pocket of my robe for my glasses. Damn. They were upstairs on the bedside table. I couldn't find the light switch, so I curled up on the sofa in the blurry darkness, pushing hair away from my eyes. I realized my face was wet.

Zazie was talking. What was she saying? I tried to focus. She was talking about a book.

"It's on *The New York Times* bestseller list, written by a neurosurgeon dying of lung cancer."

"Za, I can't read that . . ."

I still called her by her pet name. We had remained friends since that first day at school in Japan. She had borne witness to the earliest days of my love story, and after Pete and I broke up, she cried with me on the phone. Over the years she'd listened patiently as I ran through endless speculations about what might have been. When the miracle of our reunion happened, she was the one person who truly understood.

When Daniel and I got married, she wrote, "It's the greatest love story I've ever seen."

Now she was flailing, trying to find the right words. I was in a fetal position, cradling the phone to my ear. To ease the pressure or to lift the sorrow, she tried a different tack, telling me about a new project she was launching.

"That's brilliant," I said, feeling lost and small. She was taking on the world, while mine was crashing down.

I could tell she didn't know what to say.

"Za, I don't know what to do. Everything is black. I can't see anything ahead."

She paused for a long moment before she answered. "Just love him," she said.

Loving Daniel was my condition. It was as easy as breathing. I felt my body unclench, my pulse slow.

"I can do that," I said, exhaling.

The Ridge

Dear Shelley,
We were so lucky at CA, those views of the harbour and mountains. I want to know what you remember. I want to know everything.

I READ SOMEWHERE that lasting memories are formed when highly charged nerve cells fire during pivotal experiences. Since receiving his first email, my memories had taken flight, filling my thoughts, changing the present. Everything different, overnight.

In his second email, Daniel asked if I remembered our first encounter. Yes, I responded, absolutely. But we remembered two different things. He wrote:

You ran into me in the hall on the second floor at that ninety-degree turn by the bathroom. Literally ran into me. You were with some people, talking and not looking where you were going, and ran into me

> so hard you almost fell and I had to hold you up by your elbows. I remember thinking "hello, who's this?" as I held you up (you were light as a feather) and saw those beautiful eyes. Others were scrambling to pick up your things while I had my moment, and then you were off your way, me mine.

I plunged deep into an ocean of memories and wrote out the scene in my head. I foraged for fragments, real or invented, until I could picture it clearly.

> *The corridor is lined with lockers. I'm looking around trying to find the right classroom; then he hits me sideways and I stumble. Books fly, pencils, comb and lip gloss skip across the wooden floor. He's holding me by the elbows. Too embarrassed to return his gaze, I stare at the frayed sleeve of his jacket and hope he won't notice that I've turned flaming red. I'm the new girl, so he doesn't know me, but I have seen him before.*

I was forty-six years old, but I still blushed when I remembered him as he was then. And I was fascinated by who he'd become. He wrote that after abandoning his music career, he'd become a restorer and replicator of the painted interiors of historic homes and buildings. He spent hours, days, weeks, months scraping away the overpaint and dust and grime of centuries, searching for the gems that lay underneath. Then he would stabilize and restore the original design, filling in the missing pieces. Sometimes he had to imagine what the artist intended and fill in the blanks. He knew what layers were needed to paint an undercoat, to create a colour that looked aged yet true to the original. He'd worked on the Library of Congress, the U.S. Capitol Building, and many state buildings, churches, cathedrals and private homes.

Restore: *to bring back to a previous state; to reinstate; to take something back to its original condition.* Could we?

That was what we set out to do, unknowingly or unacknowledged, as we continued to write to each other.

"Who was *that*?" I ask Celia, who is helping me gather my scattered things after I smashed into Pete in the hallway.

"Oh, that's just Pete. Danny Peterson. Making one of his rare appearances."

There's more I'd like to ask, but she's on to the next subject, a tall blond guy who smiles at us as he walks by. "That's John, he used to date a girl from Stella Maris. That's Bill, he's president of the senior class. Oh, there's Brenda. Let's go."

Because of Celia, I am learning the ropes of campus life. "For god's sake, don't take that," she whispers to me in the lineup at the cafeteria, pointing at what appears to be some kind of meat loaf. "Just grab the dessert and we'll make ramen in our room."

Someone "accidentally" jams me with her tray before moving to the end of the food line.

"Who was that?"

"She's a total bitch, ignore her."

On Friday afternoon, at the end of the first week of classes, the dormitory is deserted. Most of the boarders have family within hours of Kobe and don't stay at school on weekends. Flopped on my bed, staring at the stains on the ceiling, I feel a little sorry for myself, homesick, at loose ends.

Brenda and Celia appear in the doorway. "C'mon, we're going downtown."

Their families live in the Northern Mariana Islands, two thousand kilometres away. Brenda is Chamorro, native to Saipan; Celia is American. They've been boarding at CA for years. The dorm has become their real home, and they've decided to adopt me.

We walk down the steep mountain road to the village of Rokkō. The main street has a soba shop, a variety store, and a bar with large paper lanterns hanging outside advertising Asahi beer.

"Three hundred yen is a dollar," Celia explains at the train station, pulling out enough for a ticket.

The train is packed with end-of-week commuters: businessmen released from the office and headed to the bars downtown, mothers carrying babies on their backs in a folded cloth sling and clasping the hands of children in bright yellow caps and school uniforms, and older women carrying *furoshiki*, cotton shopping bundles smelling of fish, onions, daikon radish and lotus root. A group of schoolgirls cover their mouths, giggling as we pass them in the aisle: the blonde Celia; Brenda, who looks like a Polynesian princess; and me. We take the last seats, at the end of the car, just as the train starts moving.

"So now you've checked out the goods, what do you think?"

"What do you mean?" I whisper, thinking her comment might sound rude to anyone who understood English.

"I'm talking about school." Celia laughs. "You know . . . *goods*. Have any of the boys caught your eye?"

I roll my eyes. "I wish."

The train moves past suburban homes, small and tidy, then along an expanse of concrete city buildings. I haven't seen Pete for a couple of days. I wonder where he's been.

"*Sannomiya, Sannomiya eki de gozai masu*," a female voice pipes through the loudspeaker.

"That's our stop."

"Stick close," Celia orders as we move into the bustle. Outside the entrance of the train station, street vendors hawk baked yams, barbecued octopus and eel from wooden carts. Across the street, the buildings flash neon signs and moving projections that look futuristic.

"Wow!"

Brenda and Celia exchange glances, enjoying my reaction. "You haven't seen anything yet."

We enter a warren of covered streets that seems to go on and on, polyglot signs in English and French as well as kanji, advertising coffee shops, soba shops, Parisian bakeries and Italian pizza parlours, bars and boutiques filled with designer knock-offs and accessories. We pass a music store with swinging chairs hanging on chains, displaying *Fragile* by Yes in the window. A movie theatre is running *The Godfather*.

Women in kimonos and getas shop alongside women in miniskirts, as if different centuries have been superimposed. Brenda laughs, watching me take it all in.

I stop us and say, "First, I have to have a *real* cup of coffee."

"Done."

"Then let's go for a pizza."

"Okay."

"Oh, wait, look at that cute dress in the window. Can we go into that shop?"

All at once, a year in Kobe doesn't feel like a hardship.

"The Japanese really can't tell our ages," Celia says later, and she orders a beer.

Brilliant.

On Sunday the campus is dead quiet and the long ridge of the mountain is ours. We blast music as loud as we like, sleep as long as we want. When we leave our rooms, there are places to sit and read or write letters, beneath the tall spruces or up the creek by the graveyard. Pathways lead to clearings where wild azalea grows. There are hidden spots where couples go to make out, secret places to be alone. I lean against a moss-covered boulder, take out a piece of thin blue airmail paper and begin my first letter home.

On Monday Celia is gone before I get out of bed. I'm late again, racing to the cafeteria to grab a plastic mug of boiling water to take back to our room, where I now keep a jar of Nescafé.

The day students begin to arrive, climbing out of expensive

black cars driven by chauffeurs, or sweating after the steep climb from the train station.

Will he show up today?

A girl with a thick German accent whom I've seen in history class waves as she walks by with a Japanese guy. The student body is like a package of licorice allsorts. There are children whose White Russian grandparents had fled to Shanghai after the Bolshevik revolution and then had to escape once more after Mao's revolution, making their home in Kobe. There are South Asians such as DJ, whose father owns the best Indian restaurant in the city, and Chinese like the Tam brothers, sons of a Hong Kong millionaire. There are kids whose families fled the coup that toppled Sukarno in Indonesia. Australians, Austrians and Americans, children of every nation, their parents diplomats, members of the armed forces or part of the business community. There are Hindus, Muslims, Buddhists and Catholics. Outnumbering all these are the children of evangelical Christians. In our dorm there are girls named Faith, Hope and Charity. Seriously.

Then there are the children of mixed marriages, such as Yvonne Pearson, with her thick mass of hair, freckled nose and slightly almond-shaped green eyes, whose grandmother is Japanese. Yvonne is the only Canadian student besides me. So many stories of geography and destiny that have brought us together for a short while.

Summer lingers late in Japan. The weather is sticky and sultry. After class I am heading back to the dorm to change into something cooler, when across the green I notice Celia talking to Pete. I haven't seen him for days, and my heart pounds at this unexpected opportunity.

Celia sees me and waves me over. Finally, a chance to talk to him. When he notices me, he doesn't smile. I change course and head for the library.

I ask Celia about him later. "That guy you were talking to . . ."

"Pete?"

"Yeah. What's he like?" I flop onto my bed.

She looks up from the book she's reading. "He's okay. From Kochi."

"Where?"

"A city in Shikoku. He speaks a weird dialect of Japanese. His parents are missionaries. Why?"

"Whenever I see him, he seems kind of hostile."

"Pete? Nah, he's just not interested in school."

I flip over onto my stomach, feigning nonchalance. "Maybe he thinks he's too cool for the rest of us."

"No, it's not that. He lived in the dorm until this year and he always hung out with us, but his parents have just moved to Kobe and now he lives with them. He hates it. Spends most of his time in Kyoto."

"I saw him with a girl."

"That's why he spends his time in Kyoto. His girlfriend graduated last year and is there studying pottery, waiting for him to graduate so they can go to college together in the States."

"Must be serious."

Celia looks at me strangely. "Do *you* like him?"
I roll my eyes. "As if."

× × ×

Dear Daniel,
Seven days ago I found you, and in such a short time I've found a reconnection with you and my past, and a person to share thoughts and ideas and dreams and memories with, all at once.

I dreamt of you last night. I'm not sure, dreams are always so fragmented, but you were definitely there.

Dear Shelley,
Has it only been a week? Memories have been galloping through my mind like raging wild stallions, trampling all my protections.

I am enjoying this so much I may bury you in letters.

Timelines

IT HAS BEEN three months since he died. The endless summer, the distant laughter of children in the park, the searing sunlight that made me stumble and hide in the shadows, the wet, suffocating heat, topped off by an infestation of hornets and wasps that have inhabited our willow tree like some biblical plague, and that has driven me out of shock and into self-pity. I can no longer take refuge in the garden I've been working on for Daniel.

But, like all things, the summer is finally turning. September has brought some relief. The days have become shorter, less of a haul to climb through, though I hardly leave the house. It is my haven. It's my prison. Every corner of every room is infused with him. There are his samurai sword guards sitting atop his *tansu* captain's chest, his woodblock prints hanging on the wall, his guitar leaning against a chair. Like the blue box that holds our emails, every room is a memory box.

For years it was *our* house, just like the song. Cats curled up at our feet, laughter ringing through the rooms, the aroma of his cooking greeting me at the door, our fingers entwined as we entered sleep. It was here, in these rooms, that we rediscovered each other in body and, finally, in the nakedness of illness and death. But first we rediscovered each other in words.

I rushed home from work each day and dashed up to my computer. He captivated my thoughts and infused my cells with new energy. I checked my inbox again before bed at night and first thing in the morning.

There he was. His words met mine, posed and answered questions, danced and twirled on the screen. I began to print out our emails so I could take them to bed and pore over every word. Some of his stories unsettled or hurt me, made me jealous of women he had loved, of the time we had not shared. My own words sometimes surprised me; what I chose to reveal forced me to see my life at a distance. I deleted the boring, erased the mundane, distilling my stories into the memorable or the transformative. As I took command of the narrative of my life, I wondered who was this person I was composing for him. Who was the person he was promising to me?

Life on three timelines is an intricate composition. We wrote about our time in Japan, the years since, and the here and now. Our stories intersected here and there: we had come within a few miles or hours of reconnecting when I was travelling or he was touring with a band. We discovered a crisscrossed set of paths and missed opportunities. *We almost . . . Might have . . . What if . . .*

Almost immediately, a fourth timeline started to emerge. A wispy, barely uttered *maybe.*

× × ×

Leaving Mrs. Uno's Japanese class for beginners, I brush past Pete, who is leaning against the door jamb. I pretend not to see him.

"*Konnichiwa, sensei,*" he says, bowing to Mrs. Uno as she exits the classroom. Normally reserved, her face breaks into a smile.

"Ah, Pete-*san*!" She gives him a pat on the shoulder. They speak for a while in English and Japanese. I walk across the hall, open my locker and, slowly rifling around inside, eavesdrop. Though I can't understand much, they are using the familiar speech form, like old friends. He hands her a book and bows again.

After they say goodbye, he walks straight towards me. A burning sensation starts in my chest and rises to my face. When he walks past, my stomach rolls like a choppy wave in the wake of his disturbance.

Tuesday is bath night. Someone comes into our room to announce that the *ofuro* is ready. The steamy room is full of girls getting undressed, filling buckets with water to wash with before they enter the bath, in the Japanese tradition. Some girls are modest, covering themselves with wash towels. Others are exhibitionists. We are every shape and size: budding breasts, voluptuous curves, slender limbs and thunder thighs. I am boyishly thin, not like the girl I saw with Pete, who was built like a *Playboy* centrefold.

The scalding bathwater eases muscle and mind and I slip into fantasy. His hands move up my bare legs to the untouched place, the ache deep inside. Hovering above me, his lips brush mine, tongue separating them and probing.

Someone tells a joke and everyone laughs, bringing me back to the *ofuro*, the steaming realm of girls.

One school night in the dorm, I'm surprised to hear my name called.

"Shelley, phone call."

Who would call me? There are no phone lines from Beijing. My Toronto friends couldn't afford a long-distance call. I go downstairs to the public telephone in the lobby, hoping against hope it might be Pete.

It's Zazie, who lives off-campus with her parents, inviting me to her house for the weekend.

After school on Friday, we take the train to Ashiya, a city between Kobe and Osaka that overlooks Osaka Bay, known for its upscale houses and popular as a residence for foreign businessmen. Her house is deceptively plain, a low-slung modernist design of cedar and pine, but when she opens the front door, I gasp.

A waterfall flows beneath the living room floor, exposed by glass panels. Woods and gardens fall in tiers around us, framed by sliding glass doors. I've never seen anything like it. Hanging over a sofa is a massive oil painting, an exquisite still life of lotus pods in a Japanese basket emerging from a recess of dark brown and purples.

"Beautiful."

"That's one of Enid's paintings."

"Who's Enid?"

"I am." A tall woman in a Panama hat strides into the room.

"Shelley, this is my mother."

Zazie is two years younger than me, with the face of a Botticelli goddess. Enid Munroe is all angles and bangles, her dark hair falling straight to her shoulders. She takes a drag on her cigarette and looks me over.

"Come over to the light and let me take your picture. You two look good together." She commands us to sit by the window, where we pose until she is happy.

My parents are young, open-minded and cool, but Zazie's are worldly and artistic. Her father, Harry, is a businessman who recites a poem he has written after dinner. "My role is to support this matriarchy of artists," he says wryly.

We are sitting among life-size hand-painted dolls propped up on chairs, made by Olivia, one of his four daughters. Zazie is the youngest, and since her three older sisters are living in the States, I am adopted as a surrogate.

"Let's go travelling and discover the real Japan," Zazie says on the train back to school on Monday. We've already agreed to be friends for life.

× × ×

Grief has a way of distilling life, of measuring it differently. I'm digging through a basket filled with letters. The basket came from the farmers' market in Kyoto—some of the wicker spokes are broken now—and it is filled to the brim. Zazie and I have corresponded for years through ink on paper. Together we have examined our lives, the paths taken, and the markers along the way.

My gift for her wedding was a cherrywood box filled with copies of the letters she'd sent me after Japan. On the card to accompany them, I wrote: "To my most beloved friend, as you enter a new phase of life, I give you the gift of your past."

After Daniel died, her letter to me arrived by post, the old-fashioned way. She wrote: "Of all the things that have happened, this is by far the gravest. Daniel and I share the origin, we fell in love with you in the same place."

Black Bird

AFTER A FEW months of near solitude, Kirsten convinces me to take a walk with her in High Park.

The last time I came here, just before Daniel got sick, a black bird swooped down and startled me—landing on my head, sharp claws in my scalp, fluttering wings, thunderous heartbeat—before it flew off. I wrote about it that night in my journal, wondering if it was a dark omen. Or maybe I'd walked too close to her nest.

Today, in this park of happy childhood memories, I see missing friends everywhere. I used to walk these paths with my friend Ed, discussing film and philosophy. Now he is gone, felled by cancer.

There's a horn toot, signalling the little train that runs through the park, coming round the bend. Rob, my university boyfriend, drove the train as a summer job. Cancer took him too. What is it about my generation? We lived as though we would never get old, and cancer has made that come true.

Daniel and I loved to walk here, along the path bordered by the tall grasses that grow in the shallows of Grenadier Pond. Through them I catch glimpses of houses on the street where I grew up, at the top of the embankment on the other side. As children we skated on this pond when it froze—something forbidden now by the city.

There was something about the way he took my hand when I told him of these things. As though he was both reaching back in time and grasping hold of the future.

"Look, a ginkgo tree," he said on one of our walks, pausing to appreciate the undulating silver leaves, momentarily transported to his own childhood.

You must miss Japan terribly, I thought.

"You are my home," he said, reading my mind.

We loved this park in all its seasons, especially in the autumn, when the trees turned colour, their leaves twirling and falling, forming a carpet of umber and red.

Gone.

My friend Ed was my first loss.

A few days after I received the first email from Daniel, Ed called. "I'm at the hospital, Shell. My legs went out from under me just like that."

"What?!"

"They found a brain tumour."

"Fuck. No. I'll be right over."

Ed was the older brother of Snaige Valiunas, one of my best friends. I'd known him since childhood. After I returned from Japan, I began a major in theatre arts at York University, where Ed was studying film, and we started to hang out.

He was a tall, cool-looking guy with piercing blue eyes who often wore overalls without a shirt underneath. He could blow perfect smoke rings. Some people assumed we were a thing, but we were more like brother and sister. We shared a secret; we were both holding on to feelings for someone from the past.

Ed's high-school sweetheart was named Kathy. She was a friend of mine too. While I was in Japan, her mother died suddenly, and she moved to the States to live with her dad. Ed never forgot her.

Over plates of goulash at our favourite Hungarian restaurant, after watching a film or sipping late-night cappuccinos at the Coffee Mill, the topic of our first loves always surfaced. We strategized ways to track them down but had no real idea how we would find them, both Americans with common surnames, living who knew where. Check the telephone books of 108,000 U.S. cities and towns?

After graduating, Ed and I launched our careers, married other people and saw each other less. But no matter how much time had passed, whenever we got together, we spent a few minutes talking about Kathy and Pete.

I rushed to St. Joseph's Hospital, wondering what to say. Ed was the person I most wanted to tell about the miracle of finding Pete, but how could I share this news now, with all he was facing?

We talked about his upcoming surgery, the unexpected, shocking insanity of it all. We talked about life, work, family and friends.

After a while, he said, "There's something you aren't telling me."

I hesitated, felt myself blush.

Ed looked like a Buddha with his newly shaved head. His blue eyes twinkled and he smiled in his knowing way. "You found Pete."

That spring of 2002, everything seemed heightened. The last of the dirty piles of snow melted, the days grew longer, the sky more luminous. I raced through my tasks and juggled my time. I bought a laptop for Ed and took it to the hospital so he would have an easy way to communicate. The surgery had removed part of the tumour, but the pathology revealed it was cancer. He seemed strangely elated, despite his bleak prognosis. Friends he had lost touch or fallen out with were reappearing in his life. Amends were being made.

In my office on the seventh floor of an art deco building on Spadina Avenue, Deb and I were pulling together a rough cut of our most recent documentary, which followed a nurse who worked with the homeless on Toronto's streets. My crew and I were still gathering material, filming in a tent city that had sprung up on an abandoned industrial site near the lake, and at City Hall at night where some of her patients slept, lining up their sleeping bags against the wall that faced the skating rink. Using a hidden camera, we got explosive footage of the overcrowded conditions in the shelter system during an outbreak of tuberculosis.

I didn't need to be reminded; I knew how lucky I was. I had a home, a shelter, an oasis to go back to. After work, late at night, I would climb the stairs to my study. There in the darkened room, on a backlit screen, I'd met my match again.

Daniel,
In the middle of the night there was a huge fire on my street, a house just four doors from mine was burning. There were cops and sirens and fire trucks and walkie-talkies going on from three in the morning until dawn. The smell of smoke has filled my rooms. This morning I saw that the house was badly destroyed. I don't know if anyone was hurt. I've been sleep deprived all day, and this email may be less coherent even than the last one I sent you.

Did you ever want to see me again, after the last time?

Exposure

AFTER ANOTHER NIGHT spent with my ghosts, I stand in the bathroom looking into the mirror. New lines have appeared, written across my pale skin like sentences in the book of grief. Something compels me to take a selfie, pointing my phone at the mirror. Vacant eyes and harsh shadows.

Delete.

My cinematographer Mike says the camera never lies, but I don't think a camera tells the whole truth. It doesn't make allowance for the viewer's perception. It doesn't make allowance for whether the light is harsh or diffused, or for the aperture: the opening that determines the exposure.

For years we travelled the world filming suffering and destruction and life on the brink, nerve endings wired for danger, feeling completely alive. I convinced myself the images we captured would do some good, that exposing problems would invite solutions. I told myself I was compassionate. I stood behind the camera watching events unfold through a lens, telling a story that was not mine. Sometimes we wore protection: flak jackets and helmets. Sometimes I wore a black abaya. I've often been asked what it felt like to be exposed to danger, but unlike the local population in a war zone, we were prepared and protected and could leave. Danger, I already knew, arrives when you least expect it.

I looked back in the mirror to apply concealer, covering the purple shadows under my eyes.

Each of us chooses someone to reveal themselves to. Pete was my choice. In 2002, when we began to correspond, I wondered if I could again expose my heart. It had been protected for years, pumping safe and slow, a turtle in its shell. But now it had begun to race, opening wider with each word exchanged. It was a mile wide by the time I saw him again.

There is a collection of photographs from the years that follow. Our faces are lit by golden sunsets against a backdrop of ocean and mountain views. All that light blinded me. Now I see that, in some of these photographs, when I am spinning in the sun, he has a shadow in his eyes. When his heart stopped, mine was shuttered in darkness.

His gaze was the lens that defined me. Without it, who am I?

I go downstairs and stare at his garden. Only memory can pull me back to myself.

Late fall in Kobe is still hot and humid, but it's cool in the shade. In the place I go to be alone, I sit mindlessly sweeping pine needles into piles on the dirt to make circles. I am trying to picture the room where Pete sleeps. I imagine lying back on his pillow. I feel a shift, an unnerving slide from the safety of childhood. For the first time I consider the dangers of desire.

"Wild Horses" is playing from an open window, Mick's plaintive voice filling the air. A bell rings. I gather my books and walk across the green, but when I get to our literature class, the only course I share with Pete, I see his desk is empty. Again.

Mark places a black-and-white photograph on my desk, a print he exposed in his darkroom the night before. It's a profile of me taken in class, gazing off into the distance.

"I wonder who you are thinking of," he teases.

"No one you'd know." I laugh.

Pete's unpredictable appearances have kept me off balance, so I study what patterns I can find. When he does come to school, he often skips class and heads up a mountain path alone.

One day after class I hear the sound of his harmonica. As though in a trance, I track it down over moss and fallen pine needles, up the incline beside the creek.

He looks up, still sucking and blowing, one knee bent, one leg stretched in front of him. He finishes the long note. "Hey."

A Hermann Hesse novel, a pack of Seven Stars cigarettes and a lighter are on the ground next to his green army jacket. I'm intruding on his private space.

My toe makes a small groove in the dirt while I search for something to say. "Coming on the senior trip?" I ask. Our class is headed to Kyushu, the southernmost island in Japan, famous for its volcanoes and hot springs.

"Nope. Been there, done that."

The wind picks up, spreading my disappointment. "Yeah, well . . . The trip *is* expensive. I'm still thinking about it."

He studies me for a moment, then says, "It's beautiful. You should go."

Our first conversation. Four sentences. Clouds race across the sky.

In bed at night I picture his eyelashes dark against his cheekbones, his lips against the harp. It's true what they say—the eyes fall in love first.

A path of raked pebbles leads to the shrine. The Amano Yasugawara cave in Kyushu is the spiritual home of Shinto, the way of the gods, embodied in rock and stone. Mark is snapping pictures. Gregg is talking to John Low, our teacher.

Grace peers up at a massive camphor tree, said to be more than a thousand years old. "Far out," she whispers.

We gather in the shade and peer into the cavern where Amaterasu, the sun goddess, hid herself, plunging the world into darkness. The guide tells us the story: The goddess of dawn lured her out by performing a sensual dance, depicting the harvest their union would create. The world awoke to the first blush of light.

Flash. I snap out of my reverie as Mark takes another picture, and I laugh with my new friends. It has been a magical week. We've inhaled the scents of tropical flowers and seaweed; feasted our eyes on volcanic mountains, lush valleys and a turquoise sea; devoured delicious unagi and other delicacies; soaked in sulphur springs under the stars; and told each other secrets.

In a series of photographs, there we are in black-and-white. Ellen sitting cross-legged on a tatami floor. Me wearing a hotel kimono. Grace making a peace sign, blonde hair spilling over denim overalls. Gregg looking a little like John Lennon, peering through his wire-rimmed glasses.

Even after all these years, the photo album feels incomplete. When we return to school, tight-knit and full of stories, there is no sign of Pete.

Exposure: *The direction in which something focuses.*

The clock strikes two. I try not to, but my eyes settle on the patch of afternoon sunlight slanting across his empty desk. The drone of the teacher's voice goes on and on.

Exposure: *The amount of time a piece of film is open to light.*

After class I am startled to see him outside, talking to friends. So bold to show up at school after skipping class. The sun is shining, revealing gold in his brown hair.

Exposure: *The condition of being exposed to harm without protection.*

I cross my arms over nipples that have grown tight. He notices me and says something in Japanese that makes everyone laugh. I flinch. Is he laughing at me?

Now he is walking over, hazel eyes trapping me in their gaze. "How was the trip?"

"Good." I want to say more, but words don't come. I can think of nothing to say that will hold him, and after a moment he moves on.

× × ×

We pass around the album cover of *Rock of Ages*, reading the liner notes. It's a concert album, the Band's new release. There is kanji writing on the back. Someone puts the needle on a groove and "The Weight" begins to play.

We are hanging out in Grace's room, talking, as usual, about guys. They are so confusing. How to understand them, decipher or decode the things they say and do? What to make of the gestures, the shrugs and grunts and silences? It's so much easier to fall in love from afar.

We stake claims on our favourite musicians. Eric Clapton, check. Robert Plant, definitely check, though I think Jimmy Page is sexier. Someone says Led Zeppelin is coming to Osaka, but tickets are unaffordable.

I've heard that Pete plays the guitar. To me he seems as distant as a rock star, and almost as unknowable.

It's been a few weeks since I've seen him around school. I crush my cigarette under my heel and say goodnight to Gregg, after our usual rendezvous for a smoke behind the gymnasium. Walking away, I cross my arms, hugging my flannel shirt closer. It's getting cooler.

In the hallway outside Mary's room, I hear some girls talking.

"Sarah has a thing for Pete."

"Yeah, well, she can get in line."

"Isn't he with Kathy?"

I lean against the doorway. Sarah is the girl who jammed me in the cafeteria on my first day. Kathy is the girl I'd seen him kissing.

"They're together as far as *Kathy* is concerned."

"How do *you* know?"

Mary snorts with laughter. "Trust me, I *know.* Kathy is one of my best friends, and Pete's like a brother to me. I hung out with them all summer at Nojiri."

I've heard of Lake Nojiri, an ancient glacier lake in Nagano. Lots of missionary families have cottages there to escape the heat and the isolation of their far-flung missions.

I join the conversation. "What's it like there?"

"We swim and waterski and party with friends from the American school in Tokyo. There's a dance every Saturday night, and on Sunday our parents sing hymns on a steamboat." Mary lifts her eyes to heaven. We laugh.

I imagine Pete lazing in the sun.

"Kathy could have any guy she wants, but she's hung up on Pete," Mary says, shaking her head. "Fucking crazy, *baka ne*? Every one of my girlfriends has fallen for him at one time or another."

I laugh a little too loudly.

Mary grew up with Pete. It isn't the only reason, but I start to hang out with her more.

Three and a half months after Daniel died, Mary calls to see how I'm holding up. Then she tells me that her breast cancer is back. She's taken a break from her job, teaching at a primary school in rural Tennessee, to undergo treatment.

No. I say a silent prayer.

"Fucking cancer, *shitzuko*!" She still swears like a sailor in Japanese and English, making me laugh despite the devastating news.

I refuse to tell her to fight it, an expression I hate because it implies that the outcome is up to you. We commiserate over the indignities of illness, discuss her next round of treatments, and then our conversation turns to Daniel.

During my year in Japan, Mary became my friend too. Pete and I visited her after graduation, at her parents' place in Hiroshima in 1973. And we saw her thirty years later, at her home near Pigeon Forge, the Tennessee birthplace of Dolly Parton. She greeted me with a bear hug and arm-punched Daniel like a sister. They had shared so much history, from their childhood in Japan to adult life in the American South, a duality that defined them both in ways I would never fully understand.

She was a single mom living in a modest bungalow. She showed us into her living room, with its tatami floor, *mingei* fabrics, wooden *tansu* cabinets and a hibachi. Her home was American on the outside and Japanese on the inside, just like her.

Mary still called Daniel Pete, and they talked about the old days in Nashville. We reminisced about CA. She pulled out a photo album that included pictures of Pete in his twenties. I felt a pang for all I had missed, even though he was sitting next to me.

"Do you still have those photos of Pete from his band days?" I ask before we hang up. "Could you send one to me?"

She mails me two snapshots. I make copies and send the originals back to her, along with a few of Daniel's keepsakes. "Please look after yourself, dear friend," I write.

I place the snapshots on my desk. In one he has a cast on his arm. I wonder how he broke it. On the back Mary has scrawled, "Man, he was good-looking." I flash on our conversation all those years ago, that night in the dorm. *Every one of my girlfriends falls for him at one time or another.*

Had she felt that way too? How much remains hidden? How much do we ever expose?

When Daniel and I began writing to each other in the spring of 2002, we did not send photographs, relying instead on blind faith.

Dear Daniel,

I've been waiting for this moment all day. It's like a secret rendezvous, an appointment with a therapist, a time to confront myself, and most of all to receive words from you. It's a trip back to that perfect cusp of time before we made all our serious mistakes. It's also kind of scary because the man I'm writing to is really a stranger.

Dear Shelley,
I know you think I'm a stranger, but I'm the same "Pete" you knew when. A work in progress to be sure, but I really am only a fulfillment of the Pete you knew in your past. I was quite the raw nerve in a breeze in those days, wasn't I? I wonder how you remember me from Japan. Do you remember talking? Do you remember that first kiss? I do.
I knew I was in danger. Exposed and naked. All in.

Endings and Beginnings

LIFE HAD ACCELERATED in the spring of 2002, yet it seemed more weighted. *Street Nurse* was in postproduction, a film about Iraq was in the research phase, and a long-lost love was being rediscovered on my computer screen.

In the mail came an invitation to Zazie's wedding. My beloved Za had finally found the man she wanted to marry, and their wedding would take place in the Hamptons in June. I'd recently seen her in Toronto. She had come for the opening of *YES Yoko Ono*, the landmark exhibition she'd curated for the Japan Society Gallery in New York, which had moved on to the Art Gallery of Ontario.

We walked into the gallery arm and arm, like we always did, marvelling at where we found ourselves. The night before she'd attended the premiere of my feature-length film *A Child's Century of War.* We were at the zenith of our careers, but something was missing. At least for me.

At the entrance to the exhibition was Yoko's Wishing Tree. I wrote my wish on a paper tag and tied it to a branch.

"It's a miracle," Zazie said two months later, when I told her I'd found Pete.

Yes.

Ed's prognosis was bleak. He asked me to film the last year of his life. I said yes, but I was in denial. He couldn't die. Not when everything was blooming.

Like the fluorescent green buds unfurling on the trees, the emails between Daniel and me had a life of their own, insistent, not to be denied.

I wrote to him that we were getting to know each other again at hyper-intensive speed. He wrote back:

> I suspect I've frightened you with this correspondence. Please don't be frightened. I have no agenda or expectations, so when it's no longer enjoyable let me know and I will dial it back.
>
> So long till next time,
>
> Pete

But I didn't want to dial it back. I had too many questions.

"Why didn't you come on our senior class trip?" I asked him in my next email.

"I was on my own trip," he answered.

Autumn Scroll

IT IS OCTOBER, four months since he died. Yesterday I spent hours staring at the leaf patterns that flicker and fall against the living room wall. When I woke up this morning, I felt a shift. The protective shell of shock is cracking, and anger is seeping in. I want to wipe away the trauma of the past year, the pain, the vomit and physical disintegration, the lists of appointments and medications, chemo and radiation, the desperate need to hide the fear that knotted my stomach, rose in my throat and roared in my head, pounding and pounding—the fear of loss, the impossibility of it, the inevitability.

How does hope shift from faith in infinite possibility to hanging by a mere thread? Near the end it became a silent prayer for a few more months, for one more conversation. Now hope has transmuted again, into a yearning to hear his voice counselling me from beyond.

Friends tell me I need to make a new film. How can I explain that I can't breathe underwater, that I'm drowning. I reach for the memory box. Only his words can save me.

Dear Shelley . . .

I move my fingers across my name on the page. I feel the breath on his lips as he says it.

My friend Yvonne lives in Yamamoto Dori, a neighbourhood in Kobe near Mount Futatabi, which overlooks the Kobe Club. I love going to her house. This weekend they will change the seasonal *kakejiku*, the hanging scroll, and select one for autumn.

"*Obāsan*, Granny, remember Shelley, my friend from Canada?" she says to Kimisan, their housekeeper.

"*Ko-ni-chi-wa*." I pronounce the greeting carefully. Hello.

She smiles and nods welcome.

Yvonne's grandmother is Japanese, her mother is half, and Yvonne is one-quarter. Her parents are divorced and her father has moved to Ottawa. She and her mom live with Kimisan, who doesn't speak English, and whom Yvonne treats like another grandmother. Their Japanese conversations are peppered with English expressions. Yvonne and her mom speak mostly in English, with Japanese words thrown in. Their house is an eclectic mix of old and new, East and West, and is one of my favourite places to hang out. In the living room there are wooden *tansu* with iron handles, a dark blue sofa for sitting Western style, book-lined shelves everywhere, and *zabuton*, flat cushions, on the floor.

Yvonne is truly bicultural. She floats through every situation and seems at ease in every place. Unlike Pete, she doesn't mind going to school, though she seems to have outgrown it. She spends her weekends with her Japanese friends, who are all older than we are. Artists, musicians and designers wander into her house, wearing a version of cool that involves lots of black, adorned with sashes and scarves in ochre and indigo and *mosu gurin*, moss green.

Yvonne's mother rolls up the scroll that has been hanging all summer, a painting of blue morning glories. Kimisan hands her a scroll box from the cupboard, while Yvonne explains. "Autumn paintings have fall flowers like kudzu and bellflowers, or chrysanthemum. Persimmon is also a fall favourite. Changing the scroll is about honouring nature, which is constantly changing. *Mono no aware*: the transience of things."

Later that night, Yvonne and her friends and I have the living room to ourselves. There is talk about books, music and art, and they interrogate me on what is hip in the West. Inhaling from the pipe of Himalayan hash being passed around the room, I consider the ways my life is changing. Since arriving in Kobe, I've become a cup ready to be filled. Everywhere I turn there is something new to absorb, a sensory overload that fires the eyes and sparks the mind.

The tea that tastes faintly of popcorn.

The Zhuangzi is lying on the coffee table. The Way of Tao, the essential text of Taoism, in the immortal words of Master Zhuang. *Am I a man who dreamed of being a butterfly, or a butterfly dreaming of being a man?*

I am feeling very stoned.

Yvonne puts on Pink Floyd's *Days of Future Passed* and opens a window. One of her friends turns to me. "Pink Floyd, *sai-ke-de-ri-cu, so ne*?"

"*Honto ne*. Totally psychedelic."

"*Cu-ru*!"

"So cool."

We settle in to listen. The light is fading outside the window. The pipe is passed round again, and now the room is swirling. Hypnotized by music and hash, I am stirred by yearning.

Holding my teacup in both hands to warm myself, I shiver with anticipation. An autumn chill blows in through the open window.

The sun is slowly burning off the thick white fog that settled on the CA campus overnight. I scan the horizon. I know the landmarks now, and look for traces of what lies beneath, the shape of the trees with their changing colours, the rocks and the pathways. If only he would appear.

Caught up in the whirlwind of activities and friends, I almost manage to forget, but every morning the possibility he might show up adds extra promise to the day.

After class I steal up to the overhang where he sometimes sits. It's abandoned. There's an American aircraft carrier far below, a dot in the harbour, symbol of the relationship between two nations, conqueror and conquered, that seems to be evolving. What do the Japanese think about America's war in Vietnam, a country they too once invaded? I wish I could ask Pete. I so badly want to know him and I want to know Japan. I am looking for a way in.

We live in a cloud, up a mountain at an international school, a world of its own. But Japan is in the air, and the light, and the smells and sounds. It spreads out beneath us. It is in the cadence of words I hear without comprehension, the sentences with their unique rhythms and vowel sounds, *a*, *i*, *u*, *e*, *o*, and the way those overheard conversations are peppered with emphatic conclusions: *So ne!* Yes, isn't it! *Hai!* Yes, absolutely! *Honto ne!* Yes, true, exactly!

At the foot of our mountain, on a trip to buy cigarettes and chocolate bars and packets of ramen, Japan envelops me: the swanlike grace of women who seem to defy gravity as they teeter on wooden clogs and clutch their shopping wrapped in colourful silk *furoshiki*, the macho grunts and gestures of men emerging from the local bar. The vendor in a small shop I visit reaches for the Mars bar and Seven Stars cigarettes I point to, frowning slightly. I add a packet of pencils and a notebook to my purchase.

"*Arigatō gozaimasu.*" The Japanese words hang on my tongue in hesitation. I feel myself blushing.

"*Dō itashimashite.*" He smiles at me. You're welcome.

× × ×

How long have I been sitting here, remembering? I look at my phone to check the time. There is the last text from Daniel that I have not been able to delete.

He sent it a week before he died, fifteen minutes after I'd left our house to meet my cousin on College Street, a five-minute walk from our house. I'd told him where I was going and that I'd be gone for less than an hour.

Lynne and I sat on the patio of Gato Nero and ordered lemonade. She, like all my friends and family, was worried about how I was coping.

It was hot and humid, and the people riding bicycles along College Street were wearing T-shirts and shorts. When did summer arrive?

Before our drinks came, my phone pinged. "Where are you?" Daniel texted.

I apologized to Lynne and ran home.

Now I stare at the words, experiencing a profound dislocation. His name and his cell number displayed on my screen make it seem like he's just out of town.

Where are you? There is only one way I know to escape the despair that washes over me. I close my eyes and remember.

× × ×

Throwing on my jeans on Monday morning after my weekend with Yvonne, I fantasize, as always, about bumping into Pete. I put on a pair of silver Afghan earrings. I imagine how, confident and at ease, I will strike up a conversation. Brushing my hair, I check in the mirror to see if it's grown any longer. I'll tell him about the night at Yvonne's. I line my eyes with kohl. Then I'll mention the day in Kyoto. I take a last look in the mirror and shrug; if I can't catch his eye, I'll captivate him with stories.

You won't believe what I bought when Zazie and I went to the Kyoto temple market. I imagine the conversation.

She and I had walked to the Tenmangu Shrine from the train station. Farmers and peddlers had laid out their wares on the pavement, forming a sea of treasures: old silk kimonos and farm baskets, pottery and furniture. He would know all this, of course. But I want to tell him something he does not know—that I, a neophyte in Japan, appreciate these riches, the people, the place.

I'll describe the conversation we had with a farmer's wife, who told us about her antique jewellery box with its small drawers and lift-out mirror. I'll describe the charcoal basket burnished by smoke that I bought, along with a frayed kimono the colour of laurel. I'll explain that I want to collect items as bits of memory to hold on to. But Pete, once again, doesn't show up at school and the conversation remains in my head.

My obsession with him has me unsettled, like I'm constantly moving the dial of a transistor radio, searching for a clear channel but drawing only static.

The autumn air has brought romance, touching everyone except me. Mark is going steady with Ellen. Celia has begun to date Bill, the president of the senior class.

Gregg, holding hands with Beena, launches into me. "Who are you thinking about? You aren't even listening to me," he says, laughing, when we sneak out for a last smoke before the dorms are locked for the night.

"Who *is* he?" Celia constantly asks. Usually an astute observer, she has missed every clue. During her most recent interrogation, I insist again that there's no one. "Seriously. I'm doomed to become a dried-up old spinster." I clutch my pillow and fake sob into it until we are both laughing.

But sometimes I wonder. My parents were high-school sweethearts. My mom was seventeen, the age I am now, when she gave birth to me. She has always warned me not to do what she did. It couldn't have been easy, but she got out of Camp Six, the logging community on Vancouver Island where she was raised, finished high school at night, had two more kids, became a social worker, travelled round the world and was now living in Beijing. Any way you look at it, things turned out all right for her. She stayed with the boy she loved.

× × ×

On a warm day in May 2002, driving to Ed's cottage, I was thinking about the way young love can be the best kind, the enduring kind—the kind my parents had. About the way, if young love is interrupted, there is often a lingering, even lifelong question—a what-if.

We arrived at Georgian Bay, a place filled with happy memories, got out of the car and grabbed the camera equipment. This was the first day of filming with my dying friend, at the place he loved the best. The water sparkled in the sunlight, the expanse of the bay so vast that it looked almost like an ocean.

Ed sat in his Muskoka chair, wearing a straw hat to cover his bald head. The camera rolled as we talked. He discussed the films of Jean-Luc Godard, pronouncing him the best filmmaker ever. He told stories about his father gathering wild mushrooms to stave off hunger during the Second World War. He talked about Nietzsche and the meaning of life. He talked about photography.

He now walked with a cane. Later that summer, someone would help him down to the beach, where he would sit in meditation, watching the light play on the waves. He was in high spirits—maybe it was the drugs. His loving wife and young daughters were nearby, so he never mentioned Kathy. But, as always, he asked about Pete.

Back in the city, I had proposals to write, meetings with television broadcasters to take, application forms to fill out, budgets to prepare, money to raise. There were friends' premieres to attend, dinners and drinks. And shopping to find a dress for Zazie's wedding. But late at night I was somewhere else, reliving a long-ago year in Japan and wondering about the man I was writing to. What did he think of President George W. Bush's threat to attack Iraq? Did he remember studying Marcel Proust's *Remembrance of Things Past* in literature class? Did he know which members of the Band were still alive? What did he do today? I wanted to know everything.

Most of all, I wanted an answer to the question I couldn't ask him yet. Was he falling as hard as I was?

Dear Shelley,

I so enjoy writing that: Dear Shelley. It's like a key that unlocks my protections, and I just start letting go and I don't know what's going to come out. When I came home today, I had the urge to say "Shelley, I'm home"—you have been so much in my thoughts, I almost expected to sense some part of you in my surroundings, and I so wanted to talk. Talk about this wonderful correspondence, I was having with an old friend, an old love, recently come back into my life. Someone who wants to hear my story, such as it is, and how I am completely exposing myself in a way I have never done before.

Before I forget, any news of our friend Gregg? I remember you two being close. You were in *The Crucible* together. I remember he was outstanding, but my attention was fixated on you.

Crucible

I NEED TO visit Daniel's parents, but I don't know if I can leave the house, much less board a plane. It's been five months since he died. The Delta Airlines round-trip ticket to Asheville, North Carolina, that I bought and didn't use sits on my desk next to a ticket for a missed flight to New York. I'd wanted to be with Zazie for the opening of her new exhibition at the Guggenheim, but I did not even leave the sofa on the day of departure, except to wander through rooms, listening for something.

A footstep. A call from the doorway. *Hello?* There is no one here. It is deathly quiet in my house. I pick up my iPad, scan Travelocity and buy another ticket for a flight I won't take.

I apologize to Daniel's parents over the phone: I can't fly now, I have an ear infection. It's the same one that the ear, nose and throat doctor dismissed, saying the sensations were caused by the clenching of my jaw. Whatever it is, my ear throbs and roars. It feels like the tide pounding up the right side of my face.

A few weeks later, I call Zazie. For the second time I cancel a trip to see her. She was counting on my company for a rare weekend alone at her house in the Hamptons. We planned to walk on the sand and talk about life and the future and all the things that matter, as we always have.

"I'm sorry, I've come down with the flu," I lie. I feel desperately ill, but it's not the flu. I can't bear to tell her the truth—that I'm incapable of flying, or talking about life, the future and things that matter. I'm not coping as well as expected. I'm really not coping at all. The weekend is spent in pajamas, binge-watching a Turkish drama series on Netflix. Sometimes my vision is too blurry to read the subtitles, but the plot is easy to follow. It is a love story. I watch late into the night, until my eyes can no longer stay open.

× × ×

When the thick morning fog lifts, Kobe harbour comes into view. It's so beautiful from up here on the ridge.

I wander over to the campus cafeteria and pull up a chair next to Gregg. Of all the boys in the Gloucester House boys' dorm, he's my best friend. We sit together at breakfast and dinner and we also spend time with each other after class, at one of a variety of hangouts. Sometimes we walk down to Rokkō to buy cigarettes and snacks. If we meet by chance on the main street, we wordlessly walk towards each other and head for a bowl of steaming udon. We meet behind the gym at night to have a smoke, watching the harbour lights shine red, blue and white on the black ocean, and tell each other details of our lives. As an "army brat," Gregg has lived everywhere. I tell him about Toronto, Hong Kong and China. He talks about his new love, Beena, but I never mention Pete.

Danny Peterson—Pete, my secret obsession. I've gathered a collection of stories about him. During the four years he spent in the dorm, he earned legend status for scaling down the side of the building to spend all night downtown. When he stayed in his room, that was where the party was, because he had the best record albums. If his door was shut and Mountain was playing, his mates knew to keep out; he had a girl inside.

The Pete I get glimpses of now seems somewhat a loner. But lately he's begun showing up at school more often and has formed a friendship with Gregg. I spot them behind the gymnasium. As I approach, I hear laughing.

"What's so funny?"

"Nothing," Gregg says.

I chew the freckle on my bottom lip and frown.

They begin talking about Nixon going to China. I reach for something to say, wanting in, and find myself on the easy path of condemning Western imperialism. Pete says something contrary.

I raise my eyes to the sky, then look to Gregg for help. He does his best to take my side. "Shelley's father is a China expert."

"My mother spent her childhood in China and my grandparents were on the last ship out in forty-nine," Pete says, as though we're competing. He lights a cigarette, exhales the smoke. "The Communists destroyed the art, architecture and intellectual class of one of the world's greatest civilizations."

He is right, which poisons my mood further. To wound him, I respond with "Mao's revolution fed the starving masses and ended the exploitation of warlords and foreign powers. It's their country and they had every right to expel foreigners . . . especially *missionaries*."

He crushes a cigarette with his boot and shrugs. I watch the sunlight hit the gold in his dark hair as he walks away.

"Goddamn him, he's pretentious."

Gregg just laughs, so I turn on him. "How can you like that guy?"

It's Celia who tells me the news. "We got parts in the play!"

I run over to the academic building to check out the list. I've been given the role of Mary Warren in Arthur Miller's *The Crucible*. Zazie is cast as Abigail and Gregg as John Proctor. Grace, Mary, Celia and Brenda are in the cast too. John Low, my favourite teacher, is the director.

Racing to the gymnasium to look for Gregg, I round the corner of the building and stop short. Pete, with his back to me, is deep in conversation with my friend. I almost turn tail, but Gregg waves me over.

"Hey," I mutter to Pete, moving past him to stand on the far side of Gregg.

"Hey," he answers. I notice he's wearing a bracelet of Buddhist prayer beads and the cuff of his jacket is fraying.

I turn to Gregg, excitedly telling him about the cast and the rehearsal schedule.

Pete listens until I finish. "Good for Low for choosing something subversive," he says.

Gregg and I look at him blankly.

"*The Crucible* was Miller's indictment of the McCarthy witch hunt and the House Un-American Activities Committee. They took away his passport, wouldn't let him leave the States to attend the opening of the play in London. He was blacklisted and sentenced to prison."

I look at Gregg. All I knew about Miller was that he had married Marilyn Monroe. Gregg makes a crack about our ignorance and I laugh, but I'm smarting. I don't want Pete to think I'm shallow. He says nothing about our being cast as leads in the play. He seems genuinely unimpressed.

I can still see Gregg and Pete standing there. I remember the scent of pine in the fall air. But grief has me questioning things. Have I misremembered or invented? Have I rewritten the scenes?

My mom saved the letters I wrote to my family that year. I fish them out of the Chinese chest where I keep them with our family photos and start reading. Descriptions of Kobe, school, Zazie and Gregg and Celia and John Low fill the pages. In one dated October, I write excitedly about *The Crucible. Wish me luck on November 3rd and 4th*, I signed off. I never mentioned Pete.

× × ×

The role of Mary Warren is disturbing. She is torn between falsely accusing the wife of her employer, John Proctor, of witchcraft to protect her friend Abigail, who's been having an affair with Proctor, or doing the right thing.

We are sitting on the grass rehearsing our lines. Gregg, as Proctor, begs me to tell the truth. Zazie, as Abigail, points her finger at me, saying, "I see a yellow bird." But I have lost my focus. Pete has wandered over and has stopped to watch, one eyebrow raised.

"Everyone having fun over-eeeemoting?"

"Well, the play *is* about hysterical girls," Gregg says, and laughs.

I shake my head at the two of them. "Asshole."

About ten days after his first email, Daniel wrote this:

> Dear Shelley,
> And the Story Continues: Chapter Three, in which our bewildered hero learns to spell the word "obsession," wily womanly witchcraft, and other techniques of feminine persuasion.

He wrote about a woman he had spent a decade with, someone he had fallen hard for. Despite irrational pangs of jealousy, I clung to the fact that he was unburdening himself to me, his first real love . . . until even that illusion was shattered.

He wrote:

> The fact that you knew me in Japan is a comforting thought to me, because I shared with you what I could at the time, and quite frankly, my attic and basement were considerably less cluttered, giving you what I think was a fairly unobstructed view. I don't think you realized it at the time, but you arrived in my life after a particularly intense relationship of considerable duration (at least for someone my age). I don't remember how much I told you.

He described the girl I'd seen him kissing on the first day of school.

> She was a stunningly beautiful voluptuous feast of flesh for a youngster with hormones raging and glands on fire. We were in love, and also quite sexually adventurous.

His words stirred up a cauldron of emotions. I felt myself pigeonholed between his two great loves. I felt altered and diminished. After a night at war with my pillow, I wrote him this:

> Dear Daniel,
> Have you read *The Alexandria Quartet* by Lawrence Durrell?

On the slim chance you haven't, it is four novels constructed over the same story, the same time frame, each told by a different participant. I was blown away when I read it years ago, because it opened my eyes in an utterly new way. Which narrative was the "true" one? Which perspective was the one you most wanted to believe? And of course, the truth is that shared experience is what brings us together but, in fact, we never share the same experience at all. What I'm trying to say is that I now realize that you didn't feel the same way I did in Japan. How could you? You'd had an intense love with someone before. I didn't realize that until tonight, at least not the depth of it. And now I see our story much differently; I realize that I was more of a special friend to you than anything else. I wrote to you earlier that it was my first time in love. I realize now it was different for you.

This is our version of *The Alexandria Quartet*.

I was thinking about the fact that I knew you at the end of your time in Japan and have "met" you again now. Maybe we have connected now for a reason. It seems that if all these memories and journals and life stories and heartbreaks and triumphs get written out, entrusted to each other, and worked through, they can, in some way, be "left behind." That would mean a passage—a way to move on and say goodbye. Just like Japan. Just like the first time.

× × ×

The Crucible consumes us.

Zazie has taken to sleeping on a futon on the floor of our room when rehearsals go late. Gregg and I fall into character and recite lines when we sneak out to meet for a smoke late at night. Celia and I practise fainting spells and bouts of hysteria. One night, a group of us dance under the stars, arms raised, swirling in circles until we become dizzy, imagining the forests of Salem.

We are enclosed in an experience.

I've gone off Pete entirely. My body feels swollen at the seams from the slow boil that rises inside me when I see him. His comments have become more and more irritating. A series of brilliant "comebacks" haunt me as I lie in bed at night. I want him out of my head. Who does he think he is, anyway? He is beginning to look pale and his skin has broken out a little. Who cares if he shows up at school, even if he is showing up more often.

× × ×

Dear Shelley,

You sound so sad and you are so wrong. I don't know if I can set the record straight with you, but I feel I must. Shelley, make no mistake, I was very much IN LOVE with you in Kobe. You brought me such joy and inspired a deeper desire than I had known before. You were very precious to me, and I was tormented by the inevitability of our parting. It was one of the most romantic experiences of my life. I was devastated when we parted. You were my true love. During this correspondence the only thing I have not been completely forthcoming about is related to you because I didn't think it was appropriate, somehow, to bring up too much about the depth of my feelings for you, even though it was ages ago. In my mind, this connection was too delicate to bear the potential for misunderstandings, arising out of too much elaboration on the subject. I was hoping to get to it later, when we were more at ease with each other, more current, so to speak, but there, I've said it. I couldn't bear the idea of you thinking what you said in your letter, and I hope I haven't made you uncomfortable, but it's true Shelley, you were my woman and I was ALL yours, no question.

I feel more than a little naked and exposed right now. I am reliving and re-experiencing all those intense emotions, the deep love I felt for you. When writing, the years that have passed since have ceased to exist and I am that young man in love all over again. I keep all those memories locked away in a very safe and special place. My heart hasn't had this kind of emotional aerobics workout in a long, long time and I know things have only just begun.

× × ×

Peeking from behind the curtains into the packed auditorium, I make out faces in the front row, but everything beyond is a blur. Is that Pete leaning up against the back wall?

When the curtain rises, the auditorium falls away and we are in Salem. We become the characters we play. I *am* the weak-willed Mary Warren. Gregg—John Proctor—begs me to tell the truth. Abigail and her followers bring their hysteria to a fever pitch when I deliver the final blow. But it's Gregg who brings down the house.

We party late into the night, bonded, united, high on life, comrades for the remainder of school. It's dawn when I drift off to sleep, musing about time. A month ago, the school year ahead seemed like a long road to travel. Now everything is present tense.

There's frost in the November air, and Gregg and I are hunched against the chill. He's fishing in a pocket for his lighter when Pete appears, leans forward and lights my cigarette. Caught off guard, I hope he doesn't notice the blush warming my face.

Pete compliments Gregg on his performance.

"So you *were* there, Mr. I-Hate-the-Theatre," I say, a little hurt by his omission of me.

"Ms. Bujold." He bows.

She is my favourite Canadian actress. How did he know that?

× × ×

Dear Shelley,

I always felt that there was a strong point missed in *The Alexandria Quartet*; that one was left with the impression that all of the experiences were not only different but mutually exclusive. Of course, it makes for a better story the way it was written, but don't you think that human experience is just a little messier than that, and that the overlapping of experience is what constitutes inclusive human experience?

He was right, of course. There is always more than one version to a story, and all of them could be true. He went on to confess that he'd made friends with Gregg in order to get close to me, referring to him as "My Father Confessor in all matters 'Shelley.'"

The story I thought I knew had shifted again.

Daniel was right about something else, too. Life *is* messy. Soon I would have to make some decisions. I had been involved for years with my former boss, friend and mentor—someone I loved. But our relationship had become frustrating, frayed and tattered long before. I had been afraid to cause hurt, afraid to move on, just . . . afraid. But it was time. My emotional life now belonged to someone else.

I don't know what happened to Gregg. I've googled and Facebook searched him to no avail. I'd love to think that he's having a fabulous life and dread finding out otherwise. I've stayed in touch with Zazie and reconnected with Mark and Celia and Mary. I get emails from Yvonne's yoga studio. But Gregg is missing in action.

I fish in my basket of yellowed letters and find one postmarked Seville, Spain, where Gregg went to university. He'd written to tell me there was a poster in town of a French girl who looked like me, and he asked how Pete was doing. I don't remember how I responded. Did I tell him I had pushed Pete away? I can't go down that road of regrets tonight, or think about what might have been.

Suddenly exhausted, I pick up the notebook I've been keeping since Daniel died, scribble something about entering the fire and turning to ash, then turn off the light.

Gregg as John Proctor in *The Crucible* said, "We are only what we always were, but naked now."

It's taken all these years, but I finally understand the meaning of the play: life is a test, a trial by fire that forges us and reveals who we are. Standing in line at the airport, finally checking in for the flight to Asheville, North Carolina, to see Daniel's parents, I clutch a bag of his possessions: a scarf he loved, with the scent Eternity lingering in its soft wool; a leather-bound certificate embossed with the seal of the United States Senate, acknowledging him for his restoration work on the Brumidi Corridors; a photograph of him with the Dalai Lama at the foot of his scaffolding. I am bringing these few pieces of his life to place in his parents' hands.

The Blue Ridge Mountains rise in tiers of graduated brown, ochre, blue and grey outside their living room window. Lyle and Catherine Peterson, both ninety-eight, sit on either side of me and hold my hands. I marvel at the certainty of their faith, wishing for once that I shared it.

Their bookshelves hold a photograph of Daniel and me, among ceramics collected over a lifetime. In Japan, ash is sometimes used to make a glaze. The kiln is fired to 2400 degrees. Ash and clay are placed inside the cauldron, to merge and form something beautiful.

Daniel's father says, "You are Daniel to us now."

× × ×

Dear Daniel,

I was in southern China once and, driving past a field of sunflowers, I had the strangest sensation that it was the place where your mother was born. I went back to China in the early nineties, to research a film about artists finding ways to protest after the Tiananmen Square massacre, and I spent a few months living at the Beijing Film Academy, in the student dorm. Zazie joined me for a week. We met musicians, painters and filmmakers who were taking risks to express subversive views, like Cui Jian, who made a music video that contained a scene of an egg being smashed by a hammer.

Dear Shelley,
My mother grew up in Haizhou, not far from Shanghai by today's standards. It's odd to be able to see that timeline in the "you were there and I was over here" sense. It seems that our lives have mirrored each other in interesting ways: travel, commitment to work, similar but different senses of forward motion. When you were in China after Tiananmen, I was in the Blue Ridge Mountains watching all the news I could about China and hoping beyond hope that something good would come from all that trauma.

It seems that what we have now has a life of its own, miraculous to be sure, and mysteriously, immaculately timed. We'll just have to watch it and see how it grows. The potential is something that I can't even begin to think about, because if someone else told me about this I wouldn't believe it. I just know it is a wonderful gift, to be handled with tenderness and love.

Sunrise

HANDS TREMBLING, I called his number.

He picked up. "Hello?"

I said a shaky hello back.

"Shelley . . . My god, you sound just the same."

I was dismayed, because I could not recognize his voice. He was saying something about his cellphone, about people calling him at all hours. I concentrated on the rhythm and the deep timbre—he spoke in the husky tones of a grown man. I panicked, seeking something to connect me to Pete, the teenage boy I loved in Japan, or to Daniel, the man I'd been writing to.

Reading his stories had given me a blueprint of his life, the one I might have shared. Writing to him about my own history had been a process of self-discovery. In three weeks, we had composed almost a hundred pages, enough for a joint biography. But tonight, when I sat down, eager to read his next installment, I'd found a short message with his number. *Maybe we should talk?*

I lay on the sofa with the phone to my ear, fixated on his voice and the sound of his breathing. Trying to hear the voice I remembered. Then he said something about us at CA and I had something to hold on to. I couldn't wait any longer. It was time to unburden, to make a quarter-century-late apology.

I blurted out, "I'm so sorry for how I behaved, for the way things ended."

To my astonishment he laughed. "Do you really want to go there? God, we were so young."

I began to laugh too. "Did you just forget me?"

"No. I thought of you every time I heard the word *Canada*. You know, shut your eyes and think of the Queen."

"Bastard!" We were laughing together now.

And all at once his voice *was* his, the one I remembered. We joked about the way the gods had played their games with us, mapping our years apart, crisscrossed with a pattern of near collisions.

"After university I spent a year in Encinitas, California."

"I was in Los Angeles then, playing in a band."

"Oh my god, we used to hitchhike to L.A. to hear music!" I imagined a scenario in which I, suntanned and luscious, stumbled upon him accidently. My fantasy was about to take flight when he launched into another "if only."

"I played in Detroit and Windsor in the eighties. I got very drunk and told some musicians about you. They tried to convince me to go to Toronto."

"Why didn't you?"

"I was afraid. Besides, I didn't know how to reach you."

If only. I'd been married at the time, but I would have gone to see him. We would have sparked those embers that had never been extinguished and been right back where we'd started.

The battery indicator on my phone started to blink. I switched handsets, climbed the stairs, lay down on my bed and covered myself with a blanket. How nice it would be to fall asleep with his voice in my ear. Pete and Daniel, past and present. Sometime during that night, I started to call him Daniel.

Outside the window the sky was starting to blush pink. It was almost dawn. "Daniel, how long have we been talking?"

"All night, but I can't let you go yet. Please, just a little longer."

First Snow

IN THE BATHROOM mirror I notice the shapes that sorrow has carved on my face. I apply undereye concealer, run a comb through lifeless hair that sheds into the sink.

Today a few people will gather in my living room to brainstorm with my friend Anna Maria Tremonti, who is launching a new podcast. I will serve coffee and cookies. It's a welcome distraction and a chance to connect to my before-world. But I feel less than, minus one.

Minus one is simple math. Two people minus one should equal one. But I am less than I was before.

I ask the regular questions: "How are things? How is work going?" I smile and listen and nod, but I am not really there. Minus one means you deserve an Oscar for pretending.

It is November 19, exactly five months since Daniel died. It's also our wedding anniversary. After the others leave, Anna Maria and her partner, John Filion, ask me to join them for dinner. They have been my rocks, sitting with Daniel in the hospice, sitting with me in my garden in the days after. Anna Maria was one of Daniel's favourite people. She often asked him for his take on the behaviour of guys she was dating, and when she met John, he finally offered his approval. We were so glad they'd found each other, wanting our friends to be happy like we were.

"Not tonight," I say, hugging them at the door.

After they leave, I sink into Daniel's blue chair, exhausted by the effort to seem normal. Outside the living room window, the sky is swollen and grey. It looks like it might snow.

I hear his voice in my head. *Hi, baby. How's my girl?*

"It's our anniversary. How the fuck do you think I am?"

Whoa, your grief is turning to anger.

"No, I'm just minus one. Hang on and I'll come find you in the place where you're still living."

Zazie and I have taken the train to Uji, near Kyoto, and stepped into another age. After crossing the bridge made famous in *The Tale of Genji*, women in kimonos and getas—raised wooden sandals—shuffle along the road that the author, Murasaki Shikibu, walked in the eleventh century, dreaming of her shining prince. The smell of tea wafts through the air. There is hoarfrost on the mountain.

Zazie, whose Japanese is not yet fluent, wins over a good-natured woman by bowing low and apologizing before asking directions to Byōdō-in Temple.

Sumimasen. Excuse me. *Gomen nasai*. Sorry. We giggle, trying to follow her instructions, embarrassed by our inadequate Japanese.

At the entrance of Byōdō-in, we stop to gaze at a double vision: the temple and its reflection in a lotus pond. Monks in saffron-coloured robes move in a line along the gravel pathway, through the vermilion temple gate.

"Look!" We feast our eyes on the wings of the compound, which form a butterfly.

At the butterfly's heart we enter the Amida-do, a wooden structure that has survived fires and tempests and stood in majesty for a thousand years. It takes a moment before our vision adjusts to the darkness. A shaft of refracted light illuminates the golden Amida Buddha towering above, sitting in meditation, or *zazen*. A bell tolls. Celestial musicians, carved in wood and suspended from the ceiling, appear to dance in the air.

We are silent, linking arms in joy and wonder, as we always do. I see my breath in the air.

"Good weekend?" Pete has sauntered over.

"Zazie and I went to Uji."

"Ah, you sipped their famous tea and visited the museum of *The Tale of Genji.*"

"Yes!"

"It was the first novel ever written, you know. *And* written by a woman. It's been called a great romance, but Genji is such a flawed character."

Pete, as usual, knows more than I do. I try to best him. "Why, because he falls in love with a ten-year-old girl?"

He raises an eyebrow. "The little girl reminds him of his dead lover, and anyway he doesn't act on it."

"Yeah," he adds with a grin. "But who knows what he was thinking."

× × ×

"What do twenty-nine years look like?" Daniel asked in his next email. "What do they weigh?"

"Everything. Nothing," I replied.

He wrote, "Right answer."

It felt as though I could touch him through the page. Senses heightened, body alive, I scarcely recognized myself. The slump in my posture was gone and I was becoming lithe and agile again. I needed to stretch, move, dance, jump up and down, impatient for his next words.

During our correspondence, we had skated on thin ice a few times, emotionally vulnerable, then pulled back to firm ground. But neither of us wanted to lose the connection. We had been rediscovering each other, and we were about to rediscover ourselves. After a spate of emails describing the years we had spent apart, he wrote: "Next, I give you my childhood."

> Dear Shelley;
>
> Because I've come to believe that the shape of my childhood really has its roots in my mother's childhood in China, I'm going to start there. My mother was born in China in 1921 and grew up in a walled "compound" with two other foreign missionary

families, a sort of medical facility, frequently armed guards and many servants.

My grandfather, although unfortunately indoctrinated into the "White man's burden" philosophy of cultural imperialism, was nonetheless a bit of a character, imbued with that old-fashioned evangelistic zeal born of the tent revivalists in his native North Carolina. He was an uncompromising Bible Christian of the old stripe. He was definitely a "*Daren*" (big shot) in the community, and took to the role with patriarchal vigor, dispensing massive doses of Christianity at every opportunity. He was fearless and used to travel from outpost to outpost on his Harley-Davidson motorcycle, risking contact with bandits, Chinese, Communist, and later Imperial Japanese Army. Several of my distant relatives were taken, held for ransom, or killed by various bandit groups, so it was a very real threat.

My grandmother was one of the gentlest women I've ever known but had a spine of steel when it came to all things religious, and she raised my mother to be an "Old Testament" Christian who knew her role in the family, church, and later mission. I don't think there was ever any doubt in my mother's mind about her future; that she would marry a missionary and "live in the field" was probably a foregone conclusion.

My mother came to the U.S. to attend Wheaton College, where she met my father. They married and

> went off to Yale Language School to study Chinese in preparation for going "back" to China as missionaries. In 1949, my parents left for China, but during the crossing, the Communists managed to defeat the Nationalists, so they stopped in Kobe, Japan, and there was my grandfather on the pier, with my grandmother at his side. They had escaped from Tien Tsin on the very last US Sixth Fleet ship, and he had watched the city burn as he sailed to Japan. He had managed (I still don't know how, because this ship was crammed with refugees) to convince the captain to take his automobile onboard, so he and my parents drove through a Kobe that had been for all intents and purposes flattened by US air raids during the war, to a mission house near Rokko, where my grandparents would remain.
>
> My parents eventually committed to staying in Japan, studied Japanese, and moved to Kochi in Shikoku.

It is a colourless day, sky sullen with the hint of approaching winter. Gregg pulls his scarf tighter around his neck. The ocean is flat steel, and the ships in Kobe harbour look like toys placed on a board far below us.

Pete and I are arguing, with Gregg standing between us like a sentry.

"Why come to someone else's country and try to convert them?" I provoke him.

"Christians have a lousy conversion rate in Japan," Pete says, as though that makes a difference, adding, "The Japanese mostly ignore them."

"Yeah, but—"

"They offer rice in exchange for souls and only snag a few lonely converts. I should know—it's the family business."

"My parents are agnostic. We never went to church," I say, skipping the fact that when I was young, I wanted to go to church because my friends did. Once I tagged along with a girlfriend's family, getting up before my parents and skipping breakfast. In St. James Cathedral, already light-headed and then subjected to excessive sitting, standing, and kneeling, I blacked out. When I came to, I was lying on a pew looking at angels on the ceiling.

Shaking the memory, I press on. "Proselytizing people in their own land, who have their own spiritual beliefs, is imperialistic."

I don't know why I'm picking this fight, when my own family history is one of privilege and exploitation. My great-grandfather had a stint as clerk to the Indian agent at the Crooked Lake reserve in Saskatchewan before leaving to open a movie theatre in nearby Broadview. He was part of the system that stole Indigenous children from their parents, stripped them of their language and culture, forced them to pray to a white man's god, abused and sometimes let them die alone at residential schools. There are enough ghosts in my family closet to reckon with.

Still, I feel like arguing with Pete. "Pushing your faith on others is unconscionable."

Pete considers for a moment. "It's not that simple. For people like my parents, it's not about conquest but about serving. They admire the Japanese. They speak the language. My parents have lifelong Japanese friends who will never share their beliefs."

He takes a drag on his cigarette and pauses to blow out the smoke. "My mother's parents were missionaries, so it's bred in the bone. My father's a little different; he paints and gardens and finds Japanese culture very inspiring. Enlightened, even."

"Then why does he want to change it?"

"When he was twelve years old, he went to a tent revival and heard God call him. Literally *call* him. He sees this as predestination."

I shake my head.

"On my twelfth birthday, I refused to go to church anymore. My parents spent years devoted to saving souls and then their youngest son rejects it all. Maybe they were tired, but they didn't force me."

"I'm sorry, I didn't mean—"

"Things are not always what they seem, Shelley. Nor are people." He looks me straight in the eye and then glances up. "It looks like it might snow."

× × ×

Dear Shelley,
Kochi had been bombed extensively during the war. My parents built a house in the old part of town, across the street from a shiitake mushroom factory, which had been bombed to pieces. This was one of my playgrounds as a child; ruins of a factory that dated back 200 years, nothing but foundations and crumbling old transitional Japanese buildings that would slowly melt in the rainy season. We were the only foreigners in a city of 250,000, so everywhere I went I was tormented by Japanese schoolgirls who thought I was considerably more interesting than the blue-eyed blonde-haired dolls that were all the rage at the time.

People would stare and I learned to get used to it, but I was always aware of the attention and took to wearing hats to hide the color of my hair.

Shelley, I can't tell you how obnoxious the constant staring, pointing and attention can be. It was something I had to constantly block out, and that couldn't have been too healthy for a young boy. I had many friends in the neighborhood; of course, all Japanese, and they accepted me as one of them, so I grew up thinking I was Japanese, except for the "*gaijin*" treatment from strangers.

I attended Japanese school. With the effects of the war still painfully visible in and around the city, it was quite a big deal at the time, and I became the first foreigner to be accepted into the Kochi public school system. It turned out to be the key to becoming invisible.

My own childhood was emerging from the recesses of memory, coming into sharper and sharper focus. Strangely, our stories had many parallels.

Dear Daniel,
Like your parents, my father attended Yale language school to learn Chinese. By the time I was eleven, he was a junior professor of Chinese history at the University of Toronto, and his students, all those long-haired dope-smoking types, would sit cross-legged in our living room discussing Mao's revolution. In 1967 he won a Ford Foundation Foreign Fellowship, which meant he could take a year off and finish his doctoral thesis. We packed up and we went to Hong Kong, the closest he could get to mainland China.

The Cultural Revolution in China was in full force, as was the Vietnam War. Some of the violence had spread to the streets of Hong Kong, where the British Army patrols regularly detonated homemade bombs left by local communists. We were warned not to kick any odd-looking packages lying on the sidewalk on the way to school. I attended a British school, wore a uniform, and made friends with classmates from the States, Britain, India and Australia.

Hong Kong in 1968 seemed exotic, romantic and troubled. It was the centre of Asia, or so it seemed to me, with all the foreign news bureaus based there. My mom got a job working for Stan Karnow of *The Washington Post*. He was a character, larger than life, loud and short-tempered and gruff, but he liked my parents, and my mom had him in the palm of her hand in no time. We settled in. Hong Kong pulsed with life, crowded, noisy, filled with smells new to me, from the fishmongers to the wafting aroma of mouth-watering chow mein. The streets teemed with vendors and rickshaw drivers, narrow alleys were filled with coloured silks and knock-offs of music albums, the constant cries of haggling vendors mixed with "Sunshine of Your Love" by Cream, and on the main streets big department store windows displayed Twiggy-inspired fashion in bright pink and orange.

When I turned thirteen, I got my ears pierced, rolled up my school skirt at the waist to make it shorter, and started to wear "Slicker," the ubiquitous lipstick of my idols. I desperately wanted to be older. I envied the beautiful, glossy-haired young Chinese women meeting their lovers. Some were on the arms of American soldiers on furlough from the front lines.

With the siege of Khe Sanh and the Tet offensive in Vietnam, the horrors in China, the assassination of Martin Luther King and Robert Kennedy in the States, I developed a social conscience and joined my

> school's debating society. I was not a great debater; I got too impassioned and then couldn't think clearly. Once I decided what was wrong was wrong, I totally dismissed the notion of grey areas. All around us, in shantytowns up and down the island, was evidence that life was not fair. Corpses from China started to surface in Hong Kong Harbour, bodies of people who had been tortured in China and sent downstream. I realized how close we were and yet how far removed from the horrors behind the "bamboo curtain." The American aircraft carriers in the harbour made the war in Vietnam feel very close. I was learning the world was a big, complicated mess.
>
> Hey, my Japanese schoolboy, I have to end this and go do some work.

Later that night, I lay on the carpet next to the fire, closed my eyes and fell into a daze. I was back in my adolescence, travelling through Cambodia, Afghanistan and Samarkand. From the jungles of Southeast Asia to the Hindu Kush, from lands dotted with Buddhist temples to the mosques of Islam, there was so much to see, discover and learn about, stories that would later consume my filmmaking.

Alley Cat was purring and rubbing up against me. I petted him absent-mindedly. I threw another log on the fire and let my memory movie return to the place that it always settled on.

× × ×

"Pete?"

Coming back from a shopping trip to Kobe, I almost stumble on him in the dark. He is sitting on the ground, leaning against the big rock just outside the boys' dorm. He looks a little dazed.

"Hi."

"What are you doing here?"

"We just finished playing at the school dance."

Shifting from one leg to the other, I say, "I didn't know . . ." I wonder why no one told me his band was playing. "Any good?" I ask, referring to the set.

"We could have been better."

He doesn't seem in a hurry to move, so I stall in silence for a few moments, then say, "Well, see you . . ."

"Not if I see you first."

I walk away with accelerated breath. Why was he perched there, facing the girls' dorm, as if waiting? For me? No, of course not. But he has been hanging around more the past few weeks. The other day in literature class, when I looked up from my book, he was staring at me. Strands of wishful thinking unravel as soon as they form. *He has a girlfriend, remember?* A goddess, by all accounts.

I slip off my shoes in the *genkan* and trudge up the stairs to my room, to find Celia sprawled on her bed wearing a long, flowered granny dress.

"Were you at the dance?"

"Course. Guess what? Pete and Eddie were brought in as a replacement band, when the original group cancelled."

"Oh yeah?" I feign nonchalance, opening a shopping bag to show her my new winter coat. It looks like the weather is turning.

It's almost midnight; our anniversary is coming to an end. Through the window I see them: slow, swirling white flakes.

Every year we hoped to mark our anniversary with a trip to Japan. But we put it off year after year, telling each other we would wait until work pressures eased, until we had put some money aside, until we could do it right. Japan had become a memory, not a place, that was crystallized in perfect light. It stood for all that might have been. We might have been together for forty years. We might have had children who looked just like him. We might not have missed a single day.

We thought we could make up for every minute we'd missed, but there was never enough time. The loss presses on my chest, crushing me until I bend over, rocking back and forth, cradling a heart split in two.

Something shines on the carpet. I get down on my hands and knees.

It's a guitar pick.

My thumb rubs the flat surface over and over, like a meditation stone, until the revelation sinks in. I'm not minus one. I am the keeper of his story. I am one person holding two.

A snowflake turns to crystal on the glass.

× × ×

Dear Shelley,

I had meetings all day with my banker, tax attorney and various review boards and I feel like I've just returned from Planet Moron, principal planet in the galaxy of the irrelevant. My banker, whose name is Baese, pronounced Basie, as in the Count, was accompanied by an auditor, D. Ellington. I kid you not. They couldn't figure out why I was trying so hard not to laugh.

It has been almost exactly ten years since my divorce, and I have not been remotely interested in having a relationship. I understand that most people find this exceedingly strange, and I no longer think about it. My parents may think I'm gay. I love mellow old single-malt whisky. I pay my taxes, and suffer fools constantly. I daydream.

Now I want to discover an entirely new and different genre of music. I think, now, that I want to share my life with someone I love, sometime, somewhere. Really love, and really share my life.

It's one a.m. in Toronto, I wonder if you are sleeping?

Alchemy

THEY SAY LOVE changes the brain's chemistry. Maybe that explained the light-headedness I was experiencing when I tried to focus, make my lists, finish my shooting script, press the Iraqi embassy for journalist visas for the film I wanted to make about Iraqi youth, and contact friends looking for leads: fixers, drivers, general information. There was a network I could always rely on, colleagues who worked all over the world, and we shared information that could keep us safe.

I called my friend Lyse Doucet at the BBC. "Hey, Lyse, do you know a good driver in Baghdad?"

"I've been hearing about some old high-school romance," she teased before she answered my question.

"I think I'm in deep," I told her.

"Wow. What about you and Michael?"

From the minute I saw Daniel's name in my inbox, I had understood one thing: I would not let anything or anyone get in the way of finding out if what I was feeling was real. When I tried to decipher what that feeling was, I realized that even more than love, it was hope. I had been living with a hope deficit. For many years I had existed in an eddy of Michael's emotional debris, resigned to the limitations he put on our life together, always prepared to accept leftovers. Now, with hope swelling my heart, I understood I deserved more.

A few weeks after the first email from Daniel arrived, Michael came over for dinner. Before I could find the right words, he began a refrain I'd heard countless times before. "I'm too old for you. I'll never live with you. I don't know why you put up with me."

I set down our plates of food and poured him a glass of wine. "You're right," I said quietly. "It's over."

After he was gone, I crept upstairs, shaken. Michael had been in my life for so long, as boss and mentor, then friend and finally lover. I would miss him. My stomach churned, my heart was sore, but gone was the stifled feeling I had grown so used to that I hadn't known it was there, until Daniel's email flew in from the blue.

The future suddenly seemed as expansive as the sky. I turned on my computer.

A few weeks later, in June 2002, I flew to La Guardia Airport and took a taxi to the Manhattan address we'd agreed on. There she was, waiting on a crowded street corner. Celia Oyler, my roommate at CA. I would have known her anywhere. Her eyes were the same deep blue I remembered, and her laugh was just as infectious. She looked fabulous in a black Eileen Fisher Japanese-styled outfit, very New York.

She had become a professor of education at Columbia University. In the years since high school, I'd been to New York many times but had never known she was there. Classmates.com had reunited us too. We drank and talked late into the night. We compared notes on our lives, talked about old friends and new ones. Celia told me she was a lesbian.

"But all we used to talk about was boys!" We broke into fits of laughter at how life had changed or revealed us.

"Let's call Pete!"

I dialed his number and handed her the phone. They joked and reminisced, and I was flooded with happiness.

After she hung up, she asked, "Why haven't you seen each other yet?"

I was desperately impatient to see him. Every waking minute was filled with thoughts of him. I would lie in bed at night and picture him: His hair with different shades of brown in it, when the sun hit it a certain way. The crease in his cheek when he smiled. I'd almost worn out Sheryl Crow's "It's Only Love," playing it on streetcars and airplanes or walking somewhere, the lyrics like a match set to kindling. I was on fire, ready to find out if my feelings were real, but he didn't mention getting together. I considered getting on a plane and surprising him, but I was scared to risk disaster.

Finally, he confessed. He had been in a serious accident, fallen ten feet from a scaffold to the ground, badly injuring himself, and was now a semi-invalid.

I tried to conceal my shock. "Are you in a wheelchair?"

"I'm not in a wheelchair."

His feet had been so mangled the doctors said it was possible he might never walk again. He had holed up in a cabin in the mountains to heal and prove them wrong. Now, a few years after the accident, he hobbled.

"Are you okay?"

"I'm not okay, but I will be."

He had learned to adapt to his injuries, found ways to work, but he avoided physical activity if it caused him too much pain. He said, after a little hesitation, that this had caused him to put on a lot of weight. He said his great fear was disappointing me.

I pictured the tall, lanky boy with long hair I had once known. He had already told me he had male pattern baldness, and I'd adjusted my mental picture. But this news put fear in my heart. Was he unrecognizable?

He answered the question I couldn't ask. "I'm not the boy in your photograph. I'm not the way you remember me."

I said it didn't matter, not certain I was telling the truth.

He told me our reconnection had given him new energy, a reason to push through the pain and work on a full recovery. He said he was already a new man. He asked me to give him time.

"How long?" I asked, trying to hide my creeping fear.

"Seven months."

I am by nature an optimist, believing that most things are possible, but I've never been known for my patience. I said, "Okay. Take your time."

He began to see a Chinese doctor, who treated him with acupuncture and herbs, and found a physiotherapist named Bonnie to work on his back and feet. His sessions with her made him cry out in pain.

"What's her name?" she shouted whenever he was protesting or fading.

"Shelley."

"I can't hear you! What's her name?"

After a few months, the bones in his feet had realigned and he was able to walk longer distances. Our nightly phone calls became reports of his progress. Seven months seemed interminable to me, but it was a marathon for him.

After I left Celia in New York, I went to Zazie's wedding in the Hamptons. At the dinner the night before they made their vows, I gave a toast to the bride, recalling the first day of school, when we had met and promised to be friends forever. Alexandra Munroe, renowned curator of modern and contemporary Asian art, married Robert Rosenkranz, a brilliant financier and philanthropist, in a beautiful old stone church. The nave was filled with family and friends: Enid and Harry, her sisters Victoria, Antonia and Olivia, and their partners and children, a mixture of artists and gallery owners, writers and CEOs and old friends from Japan. Yoko Ono slipped into the pew behind me.

Later, at the reception, I was on the dance floor when "I Saw Her Standing There" by the Beatles started to play.

"What's so funny?" my dance partner asked. I tried to

explain all the connections: Zazie and Yoko, Yoko and John, falling in love at seventeen, a wish on Yoko's tree. A few days earlier, Daniel had written this:

> My band in Nashville once did a cover of "I Saw Her Standing There." It was the only song I ever sang lead on. Do you remember the lyrics? *She was just seventeen* . . . Well, it took me one pass through the lyrics and I knew who I was singing about. After the show I went off by myself and got dead drunk, thinking about you.

When the song ended, I looked across the room at Yoko. How had she survived the worst thing? Who could even fathom it?

I called Daniel late that night, telling him about the wedding and some of the people he knew from Japan who had attended. I told him about the dance, the song. My head was circling and spinning, but I knew where I was headed.

It was inevitable.

Oshibana

PETE IS MY secret. My torment. My misery. My obsession. I stash away each encounter with him for further examination and revisit each remark time and again.

His eyes are like mirrors, trapping me in their gaze. His right eyebrow has a small scar like a dash through it, forming an inquisitive line. Who is he?

I often watch him from a distance, my usual point of observation. What is it about Pete that makes me react this way?

With each email, every story, Daniel came into clearer focus. I was getting to know him even better than before.

> Dear Shelley,
>
> Our school buildings dated back to the late 19th century, traditional Japanese wooden structures with an ancient smell that I can still remember. I loved my teachers and really wanted to please them, but couldn't help being a boy, and was

constantly making mischief along with my friends. When caught, we would be made to sit on the floor in the hall outside the classroom, told to meditate and find the harmony within that would enable us to rejoin the class.

My best times were spent exploring all the mysterious temples, shrines, bombed-out and abandoned houses and factories, and blazing trails up and down mountains covered in thick tropical vegetation. Buddhist monks and Shinto priests regularly invited me into their residences for tea and sweets, told me stories, tolerated my questions, and did their best to answer them with lots of laughter, long, sobering silences followed by parables that were usually beyond my young mind, but exciting, because it was forbidden knowledge.

Every so often I tried to understand what those wonderful monks meant by *mu*, or nothingness, or what kind of place the "void" was. These musings rarely lasted for very long, but one autumn day when the air had a slight "snap" and the gravel on the beach was warmed "just so" by the sun, I had an "experience," moment of bliss, rightness, perfect balance of sound and silence, hot and cold, being and not being, presence and absence, pressuring and yielding, until I heard a loud humming sound in my mind, followed by a loud explosion, and then I was back. During the bicycle ride home, watching the silver bamboo leaves in the

> wind, I was just humming and humming with sensory input. I was 11 years old and never spoke of it to anyone.

The Japanese have an art form called *oshibana*. They forage for bits of nature, all kinds of leaves and flowers, then press and dry them. These pieces are placed on a mat, rearranged and honed until a picture emerges. We were doing that with our letters, dipping into a lifetime of experiences, choosing what to reveal. As the arc of my life began to reveal itself, I saw patterns I'd never noticed before.

> Dear Kochi Kid,
> On the way back to Canada from Hong Kong, we went to Cambodia and stayed in a run-down hotel in Siem Reap. The only foreigners we saw were working for the Peace Corps. Tourists had disappeared as rumours of war began to surface. I remember looking at the jungle, thinking, "That's Vietnam, just beyond those trees; this is what it must have looked like before the war."
>
> We passed tranquil villages where children ran barefoot and animals lived under houses built on stilts. It was eerily silent in those months, before Kissinger's secret bombing campaign began.
>
> At Angkor Wat, once a vast city of temples, now a crumbling empire of ruins overgrown with jungle, we entered the remnants of shrines and edifices that

were crawling with snakes. We had the place to ourselves, except for monkeys calling to each other from above.

As though in a trance, I stood inside a former temple, transfixed by a feeling I could not understand, and when I snapped out of it, everyone was gone. I panicked and ran through a labyrinth of fallen stone, stumbling and scraping my knee. It was probably only ten minutes or so, but each second was terrifying. Then I heard my name. It was our guide, a student we'd hired from the university, who'd followed a path back to find me.

I still remember the relief I felt when I saw him emerge from the overgrown vines and trees. Years later, during the Killing Fields, I wondered if he'd made it out alive. Pol Pot had begun his campaign of terror by murdering intellectuals like him. Then all those peaceful villages, the barefoot children, their families, their livestock, were destroyed.

Afghanistan was the first Muslim country we visited. A woman covered head to toe in a black burka, with only a slit covered by a horsehair net to see through, passed us on the street, and unexpectedly whacked my mother with a walking stick. My mom was wearing a summer dress and sandals. We never thought to study the cultures we were travelling to; we just landed smack in the middle of a place, our eyes open to its wonder. We did not realize our behaviour or dress could be insulting to the people whose country we were guests in. We were so naive.

I returned to Afghanistan with Lyse Doucet to film during the era of warlords and civil war, and found a country in ruins, children who'd lost limbs to land mines, homes destroyed by rockets, a tragedy too enormous to fathom. I thought back to the days as an adolescent when I watched children fly their paper kites from the rocky heights surrounding Kabul, when the country seemed isolated in a rhythm of its own time, before the Russians, before the cycle of endless war.

All in a lifetime.

"Want to go out sometime?"

I look up in astonishment. It's Eddie Kanai smiling down at me, Eddie who plays with Pete in a band, Eddie who has never spoken a word to me.

Eddie is one of the few local Japanese kids at CA. His parents hope that a diploma from an international school will give him a better chance at getting into an Ivy League university in America. Eddie wants to be a drummer. Tall and thin, with hair that falls past his shoulders, a long nose and beautiful almond-shaped eyes, he has an unusual and not unattractive face that's a little pitted by acne scars.

A few days later I am sitting on the floor of Eddie's bedroom surrounded by record albums. I flip through the stack: Led Zeppelin, Cream, Hendrix. We are leaning against the lower bunk bed.

"You still have bunk beds?" I tease.

"The top one is Pete's."

I sit up a little straighter. "Pete's?"

"He stays here all the time."

I'm all attention now.

"You should have seen him when he first arrived from Kochi. Poor kid was homesick and spoke a dialect I could hardly understand. My parents kind of adopted him."

I'm taking this in when Eddie leans in for a kiss. I feel his tongue in my mouth, listen to a skip in the record where someone has scratched it, the floor hard beneath my tailbone. I do my best to get into the kiss, but there's no fire to ignite us. He must feel it too, because he soon gets up, walks over to the turntable and turns up the volume.

"Pete and I did a cover of this at the dance. Lucky you weren't there. We have some practising to do." He grins at me.

I pepper him with questions about the band, and Pete, trying not to be obvious. Eddie doesn't seem to mind. We get a little high and have lots of laughs and he doesn't kiss me again.

Later we go downstairs, where his parents are having cocktails. His mother is stunning, glossy black hair piled high off her long neck, and his father is urbane and handsome. Eddie is bound to turn out well. They invite me to join them for dinner at a Chinese restaurant, where Eddie and I sit side by side, talking and laughing easily.

"Thank you so much. I really had fun."

"Me too. Come hear us play sometime."

The evening has morphed from an awkward date into something better. I've gathered new insights into Pete, and in Eddie I've gained a new friend.

It's almost Christmas. The day before school ends, Pete shows up in class. He slouches in his seat across the semicircle of desks from me and makes a peace sign. At the end of the day I see him with Gregg.

"You finally come back to school just in time for it to end?" I feel lighthearted enough to tease him. I get a smile, but he's not his usual cocky self.

Gregg asks about my Christmas plans. I've been given a month off because of the lengthy travel time getting to Beijing and back.

"You'll be gone a whole month?"

"Yes. I can't wait."

"I'm headed to Spain," Gregg says and turns to Pete. "What are you doing?"

"Surviving the Virgin Birth and all the rituals the Christians borrowed from pagans. In other words, home with my parents."

We laugh.

Before we disband, Pete turns to me. "I hear you're seeing Eddie."

I want to tell him that the boy I want is standing so close I can feel an electric current up my spine. I tell him Eddie and I are just friends.

"He's a great guy," Pete says. For once, we both agree.

"Safe travels. Keep your powder dry and the wind at your back." He gives me a look that makes me blush.

The plane lifts, banks and takes off from Osaka. Scenes and images sift through my mind, but everywhere I look, I see him. His casual strut, the way he pulls out his harmonica and plays on a whim, the way my heart races with each glimpse of him. I rake through each conversation, every look exchanged. Each one, like a flower or leaf, is forming his *oshibana*.

The clouds are high above the ocean, the miles between us growing in number. For now I have enough bits and pieces to form the edges of his picture, enough memories to hang on to.

The Wait

IN THE CITY a heat wave took hold. Daniel's first email had landed in early April and now it was July. Taking respite in the shade of my back garden, I lay on the grass in a daydream.

Daniel and I spoke on the phone each night. The time between was a gap. Sometimes I was seized with doubt, wondering if the mysterious ingredients that feed teenage love might have a shelf life.

My forty-seventh birthday was approaching. Drinking margaritas with Kirsten and Susan, the tequila rushed to my head. It had to last, I told them. But before I could find out for certain, five endless months lay between us.

The summer of waiting was interspersed with filming sessions with Ed. He was becoming frail. On the drive to and from his cottage, I considered the finite arc of a life. It really did happen in the blink of an eye. Our conversations had turned from hope for a cure to a search for meaning. What meaning could we find?

Daniel, by contrast, was coming back to life. On the phone he told me he'd run up seventy flights of stairs.

"Did Bonnie make you do that?" I asked in disbelief.

"No, I wanted to test myself."

"How are you feeling?" I asked him.

"Ready for a second harvest."

I was able to rein in my impatience by focusing on the next film. In October we were going to Iraq. We'd scored journalist visas after months of petitioning the hapless diplomats at the Iraqi embassy in Ottawa. It was, as they say, a matter of luck and timing.

After 9/11, many Americans had been asking, "Why do they hate us?" At one of our weekly dinners eating Chinese and talking politics, Olivia Ward, foreign correspondent for *The Toronto Star*, said, "I don't get how anyone can ask that." She grabbed another piece of chicken with her chopsticks and popped it into her mouth.

As usual, insights we'd gleaned from our combined years of covering human conflict around the globe peppered the conversation. "Just look at Iraq," Olivia carried on. "The Americans called on Iraqis to rise up against Saddam Hussein, then abandoned them." She'd witnessed the American bombing campaign of Iraq called Operation Desert Fox in 1998, and the ongoing crippling effects of U.N. sanctions. "Despite the atrocities of Saddam Hussein, the next generation is primed to hate America."

And with that, we had an idea for a film.

In July we drove to Ottawa to meet the Baathist diplomats in person. They were very skilled at saying no. Persuading them to grant visas to film in Iraq required a promise to give time in our documentary to the effects of sanctions on children, but that was an easy one to make—it was part of our thesis. We received the prized visas in September, in time for Iraq to become the biggest story going after President George W. Bush addressed the United Nations, demanding Saddam Hussein comply with U.N. weapons inspections, setting the dictator a three-month deadline. The war on terror in Afghanistan was about to widen to include regime change in Iraq.

Time took on so many meanings during that summer of 2002. Time suspended. Time rushing ahead. Racing the clock to make our Iraq deadline. Wanting to slow down the clock for Ed. But when I was lying on the grass thinking of Daniel, time seemed like a circle, past meeting present but never seeming to arrive in the future.

And that wheel of time felt as endless as the heat wave that engulfed the city, each minute feeling like an hour.

In Search of Lost Time

> After people are dead, after the destruction of things alone, more fragile but more enduring, more unsubstantial, more persistent, more faithful, the smell and flavour are still long, like souls, remembering.
>
> — MARCEL PROUST, *Swann's Way*

TIME PASSES IN dropped stitches; I look up and there's a hole where the day was. It feels as though someone else inhabits these rooms in our house, someone else climbs out of bed and shuffles downstairs, turns up the heat. I don't recall pouring milk into my coffee, or how long I've been watching the dogs in the park across the street leaving track marks in the snow. Every now and then I find myself somewhere, wondering how I got there. At the grocery store, I fumble and fish out a debit card. I look down at the strange choice of items: chocolate bar, cucumber, bathroom cleaner. I float or glide or skate (I can't even commit to the right word;

choose any one, please, it doesn't matter) on a glassy surface without connection to anything. There are Christmas trees for sale in a parking lot. Joni Mitchell enters my head, I'm wishing *I* had a river to skate away on.

At home I pull mittens from fingers that feel separate from hands, pull off boots that seem distant from feet. Everything seems far away. The phone rings.

"Hello?" I clear my throat. I haven't spoken out loud today.

Someone at the other end of the line asks, "How are you?"

The question forces a choice: describe my paralysis or lie.

"Fine."

"No, really, how *are* you?" Now they are just being mean.

"I feel lost."

This is probably not the answer they were hoping for.

"It is natural to feel loss."

"No, I said 'lost.'"

Lost. Time vanished. Gone.

It's coming on Christmas, as the song says, but I can't face the festivities. This used to be my favourite time of year. I would drag Daniel into overdrive with me, excitedly decorating the house, shopping and cooking, dressing in velvet to attend *The Nutcracker*, wrapping gifts by the fire.

"You are like a child this time of year," he would say, and laugh. Alley Cat was batting at the sugar plum fairy that dangled from a low branch of our Christmas tree.

"Perfect moment."

That was what we always said when, overwhelmed by our good fortune, we needed to acknowledge it.

"Yes."

The corner where we always placed the tree is bare. Something punctures the numbness, becoming an itch I can't put my finger on. The feeling taunts, reaching a fevered pitch, causing me to thrash around the house, throwing open drawers. There is something I need to find.

"It's normal to have anxiety," the someone on the phone tells me. "After all, you've spent the past year in hospitals and in trauma. It doesn't just go away."

These words are meant to comfort me.

"Yes, you are right. Thank you."

After I put down the phone, I realize it was the therapist I met at the hospice, checking in on me. Did she notice I wasn't responsive? I hate to be rude.

I wander into our bedroom. Now I remember. I'm looking for Daniel's Rolex pocket watch, the one passed down from his grandfather, the one he wore at our wedding and on our trip to Paris. The one he always wore, come to think of it, dangling from a chain in his pocket. He was a little anachronistic; he treasured old things.

Where is it?

Everyone in his family said he looked just like his grandfather, the one who rode a Harley-Davidson in China. When you study photographs of Daniel and his grandfather side by side, they peer back with the same eyes.

In a drawer in his bedside table, I find his Buddhist prayer beads, his single gold hoop earring, a few tarnished silver and lapis rings and the pocket watch. The smooth surface is cool to the touch. I hold it to my ear. *Tick-tock*. It is still working, still marking time.

The undertow sucks and pulls me down. I said I'd save him. I promised I'd keep him safe and sound.

× × ×

Dear Shelley,

I was a ghost when I met you. I'd been spending my time with my older brother, who had volunteered for U.S. military intelligence rather than be drafted and sent to Vietnam. He was stationed in Tokyo, living with his wife, Cynthia. I went there as often as I could. We stayed up all night for days on end, and sleep deprivation combined with alcohol and hardly any food created the perfect environment for an exploding psychodrama that lasted months. It was us against the rest of the world—we were going to expand our consciousness—and I carried the manically expanded state with me back to school, where I basically shut out all my friends, read, listened to Tibetan chanting, meditated constantly, just waiting for the next chance to go back to Tokyo, go deeper, higher, farther out. I was an absolute wreck.

So that's where he kept disappearing to when I first arrived at school. I had assumed he was spending time with his girlfriend in Kyoto, but it turned out he had been on a trip of his own.

> I broke up with K, because she couldn't understand half of what I was talking about. Shortly after that I got a call from my sister-in-law saying they felt they should not be around me for a while. I was hurt, felt abandoned, but my intense internal life mellowed gradually to the point that I was able to notice the world around me again. I met this paragon named Shelley, fell in love, but I'll leave that story for another time. You really did save me, you know.

Christmas in Beijing is bitterly cold. The wind blows in hard from the Gobi Desert. My brother and sister and I bundle up and take bike rides along the wide boulevards and into narrow *hutongs*. Jim has taken to wearing a long padded blue coat and covering his blond hair with a Mongolian hat. Trish cheerfully calls out "*ni hao*" to the guards at the gate of the new apartment complex for foreigners, where we now reside.

We go skating on the frozen moat surrounding the Forbidden City. We shop for Christmas gifts—snuff bottles and silk robes and old wooden boxes—from the Theatre, a concession store that was once an opera house, or for fur hats and black velvet shoes from the Communist Party store for foreigners. My mom has decorated a potted plant and we place our wrapped gifts beneath it.

Each night there is a party at one of the embassies. Journalists and diplomats share our Christmas dinner. The conversations fascinate me: the coup in Chile, the counterculture movement, the disappearance of various members of China's politburo, the tensions with Moscow, the Paris peace talks. Canadian journalist John Burns has discovered a church holding a clandestine Christmas service, and we listen spellbound as he recounts the risks taken by the last remaining Chinese Christians to attend the candlelit gathering. On New Year's Eve, as the clock chimes midnight, we raise a glass to peace.

Daniel and I always celebrated New Year's Eve by putting away the decorations, cleaning the house and feasting on lucky noodles. He would make soba and a delicious lotus-root salad. I would fill a box with bits of paper, each inscribed with a word. We would randomly pull one out, and it would be our mantra for the coming year.

"*Creativity*," he said, waving his in the air. I wish he had chosen *Health*.

In 2012, when he suffered that massive heart attack, I was at my office in Toronto. I got a call from George Washington Hospital in D.C.

"Shelley? This is Dr. Reiner. We've stabilized him. Looks like he's going to make it."

It took a few minutes before the eminent heart surgeon realized I didn't have a clue who he was or what he was talking about.

"My god, has no one called you? I'm so sorry. Just a minute—I'm passing my cellphone to Daniel."

"Hi, baby." Daniel's voice was faint, and I could hear that the medical team was wheeling him on a gurney. "Don't worry, I'm fine."

I grabbed the next flight to Washington, counting the angels on the head of a pin.

Daniel had left Toronto the day before and driven to D.C. to begin a new project. He could have been on the Interstate when his blood clogged, unable to reach his heart, but he had just walked into the United States Capitol Building, with its own medical staff and special ambulances equipped with EKGs. If the doctor on staff had not called Dr. Reiner, Dick Cheney's heart surgeon, who met the ambulance when it arrived at George Washington Hospital, Daniel might be dead.

I rushed into his hospital room and grabbed his hand.

"Almost a goner." He smiled weakly.

I shook my head, unable to speak.

"But then I pictured your naked body and decided to live. You saved me again, you know."

We had a good laugh at that one.

The harsh January sunlight breaks through the CA classroom window, hitting the cover of *Remembrance of Things Past.* I open the book, settle my pens and notebook on my desk and copy today's lesson from the blackboard.

INVOLUNTARY MEMORY—in block letters, underlined.

Marcel Proust's masterpiece, the first of seven volumes, was written in 1913, sixty years ago. At first it was dismissed, then hailed as a work of genius, then forgotten, but Dr. Kriesel says it's making a comeback. I wish it had stayed forgotten. I hate the book. I don't understand a damn word. I detest Dr. Kriesel, our literature teacher. Worse, this is the only class I share with Pete. His absence disturbed me throughout the first term, but since the Christmas break he's started showing up, and his presence disturbs me even more. I turn to the correct page, waiting for the clock to strike two p.m. When the bell rings, Pete enters the room.

I try to ignore him. Our desks are laid out in a semicircle. He chooses one across the classroom, facing mine. When I look up, he raises his shirt to show his navel, a wicked grin on his face. I turn bright red. *Asshole.*

I put my head down to study the crib notes. "A madeleine dipped in tea casts the narrator into involuntary memory when a confluence of the senses, the aroma of Darjeeling tea leaves, the action of the hand automatically dipping cake into a steaming cup, transports him back in time. Suddenly he is a boy again, having tea with his aunt, surrounded by comfort and love."

I think I understand. Smells, lyrics, even the light falling a certain way can bring back moments of my childhood like a photograph emerging in a developing tray. Unbidden and immediate, a flood of memories will engulf me like an embrace.

I look up again, but Pete now has his head buried in his book.

Dr. Kriesel has a PhD in theology. A short man with thick glasses, he speaks gruffly, using words not often used in spoken language. He is, in general, terrifying. He's been a fixture at CA for years, though no one quite understands why, when everyone assumes that with his credentials he could have had an illustrious career at Princeton or Yale. Maybe that explains his disdain for our collective ignorance.

"I despair of my fate, teaching a group of hirquitickes," he will say.

I scribble furiously in my notebook as he drones on, trying to be invisible when Kriesel scans the room for his next target. No such luck. His eyebrows are raised above his glasses, pointing in my direction.

"Miss Say Well?" My name appeals to his sense of irony. It feels like he enjoys watching me stutter and burn. Pete is slouched in his chair, thighs splayed, arms crossed, watching.

"Shall I repeat the question?"

I want the floor to open up and swallow me.

"He waited for his goodnight kiss, but his mother was detained by Swann. What is the implication?"

"Umm, he might have been jealous?" I try to quell the burning in my wrists, chest, neck, face.

"He thought his mother was in love with Swann?"

"Well, yes, maybe—"

A book falls to the floor with a loud bang. "Whoops!" Pete says loudly, drawing Kriesel from me.

"Do *you* have an answer, Peterson?"

"He might have been yearning for Swann but didn't yet understand. Proust was homosexual."

Kriesel's lips curl into the beginning of a creepy smile.

My eyes follow the pull across the room, free now to fixate openly on Pete, staring in admiration as he parries and spars with Kriesel, grateful that he has rescued me.

"You better watch your back," Gregg says later to Pete.

"Nah, he likes them younger." He adds something in Japanese, which they both seem to find hilarious.

It is the first New Year's Eve since Daniel died. I'm honouring the Japanese tradition he taught me, cleaning every inch of the house. Dusting a bookshelf, I pick up Alain de Botton's *How Proust Can Change Your Life* and flip through the pages. He writes that *Remembrance of Things Past* has been retranslated and is now titled *In Search of Lost Time.* My fingers trace the words. *Remembrance. Search. Lost. Time.*

The citrus scent of *mikan* hangs in the winter air. I've eaten so many of the Japanese mandarins that my fingers are stained orange.

"Want a piece?" I ask when Pete approaches, giving him a bright smile to thank him for rescuing me in Kriesel's class. He takes a wedge of the juicy fruit and pops it in his mouth. I study his profile.

"Good Christmas?"

"It was great. How about you?"

"Was in Tokyo with my brother for most of it."

I notice he's looking pale. "Are you okay?"

His face lights up with a grin. "No, but I will be."

My yoga teacher says the present is all there is, but I'm not so certain. Maybe time is multi-layered, like shafts of light through a prism. Maybe it is circular, maybe it is infinite.

I can still see particles of dust dancing in the sunlight above his desk by the window. I still feel breathless when he looks at me. Still feel the stirrings of a love as tender and fragile as a newborn.

A bell sounds. A boy smiles. A cat by a Christmas tree.

Sitting on the floor of our bedroom, I hold time in the palm of my hand. *Tick-tock.* His pocket watch is still working. The big hand moves to meet the small one on twelve, and I remember. It's the beginning of the New Year.

Iraq

DANIEL AND I had been talking every night since our sunrise phone call. We discussed everything. I listened to the music he recommended, watched the same films and read the same books.

"We won't be able to talk on the phone for a whole month," I moaned to him. "This is going to feel like withdrawal."

My duffel bag was packed with the usual assortment of film gear, emergency syringes, Cipro antibiotics and satellite phone. I thought about what I was heading into: Iraq on the eve of a storm. The U.N. Security Council had been presented with "intelligence" on chemical weapons being held in Iraq, which turned out to be nonexistent, a false pretext for war. Saddam Hussein's regime had been given an ultimatum by the United States and Britain: grant full access to U.N. inspectors before January 17, 2003, or face the consequences.

I knew a bit about the country. I had made a documentary called *Fire and Water,* about atrocities committed by Saddam Hussein, which I'd deleted from the résumé I'd handed the Iraqi embassy. That film told the story of Iraq's former top nuclear engineer, Dr. Hussain al-Shahristani, who had studied at the University of Toronto, where he met his Canadian wife, Bernice.

Lyse Doucet had introduced us. "It's a great story, Shell."

When Shahristani refused to work on Saddam's nuclear bomb program, he was arrested and spent eleven years in solitary confinement in Abu Ghraib prison. He begged Bernice to divorce him, take the kids and go to Canada, but she refused and stayed in Baghdad, under constant surveillance by the Mukhabarat, Saddam's secret police. During a bombing raid in the first Gulf War, Dr. Shahristani made a daring prison break, and the family fled over the mountains to Iran.

When I met them, they were living in Tehran with their three teenage children and their two-year-old post–Abu Ghraib baby. They had started a foundation for Iraqi refugees, victims of Saddam's ongoing campaign against the Marsh Arabs. I travelled with them to those desperate camps, documenting their story of commitment and moral courage. Our friendship since had kept me close to events as they unfolded in their beloved Iraq.

"If we'd stayed together, you might not have become a documentary filmmaker," Daniel once said. We were always looking for reasons why fate had kept us apart.

Our film crew, cinematographer Mike Grippo, sound recordist Peter Sawade, Olivia Ward and I, arrived in Amman, Jordan, a place we knew well; we had rented an apartment there while shooting *Crimes of Honour* a couple of years earlier.

This time we were overnighting at the Intercontinental Hotel. I got to my room and called Daniel for one last conversation. We talked for a long time, hesitant to let each other go. The next morning, I was shocked by the hotel bill: the phone call had cost me seven hundred U.S. dollars.

We flew to Baghdad on what turned out to be one of the last commercial flights into the country. We checked into the Al Rasheed Hotel, walking over the face of U.S. president George Bush, tiled on the floor of the lobby, and up to rooms that were notoriously bugged. The next morning we went to the Ministry of Information, which dealt with foreign journalists. We were told we could not begin filming until a "minder" was assigned; unfortunately, none were available.

This continued for two days, and I was becoming frantic. The CBC had funded the documentary and my distributor had already made deals with international television broadcasters—the pressure was on to deliver. Olivia had the dual task of filing print stories for *The Toronto Star* while we were there, and her editor was demanding daily updates. Mike and Peter, my crew, close friends who'd travelled with me to war zones many times before, understood that this film would present the additional difficulties of trying to work in a police state, where our every move would be watched.

Eventually we were saddled with an elderly and humourless minder whose main task was to prevent us from filming anything of consequence. After a day of that, we huddled at the hotel bar, scheming how to get rid of him. Then Mike bumped into a crew he knew from NBC. They told us they worked with the only good minder in Iraq, and since they were about to leave, they introduced us to Saad, a handsome Sunni Muslim from Tikrit, Saddam's neck of the woods. Saad knew the Baathist regime's days were numbered and was banking on his relationships with Western journalists to safeguard his future. We liked him right away. He petitioned his boss and got permission to take us through the country, from Baghdad to Karbala to Basra. Overnight, the film we wanted to shoot became possible.

We filmed in madrasas where we witnessed Iraq's pivot to religious extremism. We saw crushing poverty, the effects of twelve years of sanctions, and documented in hospital wards the devastating health effects of depleted uranium on children. We drove through the rubble left by previous wars, met university students on campus and children who worked pounding metal chains in the slums. The stories of these Iraqi youth reinforced our belief that a military strike on Iraq would be a mistake on an epic scale, and that many Iraqis, already traumatized by their recent history, would turn to the very groups the war's architects in Washington claimed to be fighting.

My email romance provided comic relief to the scenes we were witnessing. We were in our beat-up van, driving the next patch of bumpy road, headed for Basra. "Shell, how do you know he's not a total loser?" Mike teased.

"Just wait, you'll see," I said.

"It's a circle," he swung his arms in an arc, mimicking a line I often used to describe our story. Peter, who never said much, cracked up.

Even Saad chimed in. "Has he sent you a photo?"

"No, but—"

Olivia couldn't help herself. Looking over her glasses, only the slightest curve of a smile betraying her stern expression, she said, "He probably didn't want to send his prison mug shot."

The van came to a stop, Mike grabbed his camera and we barrelled outside. Visible damage from Operation Desert Fox, an American bombing campaign four years earlier, marked a neighbourhood in Basra. A crowd of children noticed us and gathered round, shouting, "Down with America!"

A thirteen-year-old boy named Ali showed us a scar on the top of his head, describing the bombing raid that had injured him. We asked to meet his family, who invited us into their home. They were Shia Muslims who'd lost some family members during the Iran–Iraq War, others in the uprising against Saddam Hussein after the Gulf War, and others to American bombs. His anger and frustration brought Ali to tears. He told us he couldn't concentrate on his studies. He had constant headaches. Now the threat of a full-scale American attack terrified him. What would happen next?

On the long trip home, I thought how lucky I was to live in a country of safety and freedom. As I always did when leaving a troubled land, I felt guilt, too. What would happen to Saad and his family? Would he be safe, or more endangered because he had worked with foreigners? What would happen to all the wonderful Iraqi children and youth we had met, who'd already suffered so much and now faced more pain and death.

Telling the stories I told always came with moral quandaries. Journalists and documentary filmmakers are entrusted with the testimony of those who suffer; we parachute in to witness the horrors, then return to safety and comfort. In the end, I told myself that we were giving a voice to the voiceless, and that the world needed to know.

We laid over in London and I visited the Shahristanis, who were living in exile there. We talked about Iraq and the war that was coming. We talked about the work they were doing from London to assist Iraqi refugees. Then they asked about me.

I told them the story of Daniel, but not the secret I was holding. I had just spoken to him on the phone. He was almost ready to meet.

× × ×

Dear Shelley,

Do you remember that terraced hillside above the dam that you could see from the girls' dorm? That was my spot to go when I was thinking about you. I started spending a lot of time around campus to be around you, but I had given up on you before I even tried to get to know you. I didn't think you'd be interested in a loner like me in a million years. That is why things happened the way they did. That is why things had to happen the way they did. I needed a real love; I didn't want any more educational experiences, or casual sexual affairs. I wanted real communication, romance, tenderness, closeness, the same things I want now come to think of it.

Smash the Pot

THE SMELL OF earth damp after rain wafts in through the open window of our dormitory room. Even in the last days of winter, the terraced hillside is layered in shades of topaz and viridian. Brenda and I head out of the dorm and up the path, to the place where we always go for confessionals.

She moves closer to me, conspiratorially lowering her voice. "I like someone. *Really* like him." Brenda's last boyfriend had been busted for drugs and deported before I arrived. Everyone said it smashed her heart. I hope her new crush is worthy of my sweet friend.

"Who is it?"

"Guess. He's cuter than Eric Clapton."

Brenda is two years younger than me. I cast my mind over the boys in her class. "Is he a junior?"

"No! Come on, guess. He plays guitar . . ."

I blanch, dreading her next words. And sure enough—

"Pete! God, he is so sexy."

"But . . . he has a girlfriend."

"Not anymore. They broke up."

I digest this double hit of news: Pete has broken up with his girlfriend. I am momentarily elated. Brenda has a crush on him. There is an unspoken rule that you don't go after the boy your girlfriend has put her stake on. This is a disaster.

The next day I see them on the green. Brenda has her back to me, her shiny black hair hanging below her waist. Pete is smiling and listening to her. I make a beeline for the library.

Zazie and I decide to go travelling at February break, a perfect distraction. We take a slow-moving train. The countryside is dusted with snow, creating a tableau worthy of a Yoshida woodblock. Women wash indigo cloth on rocks by the river and fishermen navigate small barges, their poles casting long shadows on the glassy surface. Children look up from the roadside and wave.

I reach into my bag and pull out two apples, handing one to Zazie. We've been talking about school, life, art, love and the future, but I haven't mentioned Pete. Since Brenda told me her secret, I've tried to stop thinking about him. The winter daylight has waned and lengthening shadows fall across a landscape of rock and pine. The train slows at its approach to a village.

"We might be the first *gaijin* to visit," Zazie says after we leave the station and begin to look around. We are used to sideways glances in Kobe, but here people are openly staring.

"Definitely the strangest looking." We look at each other and burst out laughing. I'm wearing a padded Japanese yukata jacket on top of a long sweater and Zazi has twisted her hair up, holding it in place with a *hashi*, a chopstick.

A fierce wind has started to blow. We want to find a bowl of noodles and somewhere to stay the night. The narrow streets are lined with wooden houses, and smoke from cooking hibachis billows through the air. We spot the hiragana characters for udon on a *noren*, the curtain that screens a doorway, and pass through, entering a room with space for four customers.

"*Irasshaimase*," the owner greets us from behind the bar.

We order our meal and ask if there is a village inn. He shakes his head and points up the hill. It's almost dark when we begin our hike up to the temple gate.

A bronze bell hangs over the wooden doorway. We pull the chain. A round-faced woman opens the door, three small children peeking from behind her apron. We bow and recite the few words we have prepared: "*Sumimasen*, excuse us, please. We are travelling students. Could we spend the night?"

She ushers us inside to the warmest place, near the floor heater.

Her husband, the temple caretaker, arrives a few minutes later and greets us cheerfully. "Where are you from? How did you find our village? You are most welcome," he says in Japanese.

We look at each other with shining eyes—this is the Japan we've come looking for. Before unrolling our futon for the night, we are offered *ofuro*. The traditional bath is an unexpected luxury on such a cold night. We are shown a short path that leads to a wooden shed.

Alone inside, we strip in the frigid air. Zazie lifts the lid from the *ofuro* and the room turns white with steam. There is a heater underneath the bath.

"Are those burning coals?"

The water is scalding. I put a toe in and quickly retract it. We stand there shivering, uncertain what to do.

"Look!" Something hairy, the size of a tarantula, is moving down the back wall. We scream and jump into the cauldron.

We are still laughing about it the next day, when we arrive at our destination. The Japanese venerate their artists, declaring the great ones National Living Treasures. Their homes are places of pilgrimage, and it takes no time to find someone who can lead us to the potter we seek.

When Nakano *sensei* appears, he does not seem surprised to find two foreign students sitting cross-legged on his floor, sipping tea with his wife.

"Would you like to throw pots? *Douzo, ohairi kudasai*, please come in."

"*Yoroshiku onegaishimasu, sensei.* Thank you, teacher." We cannot believe our good fortune. We are taken to a wooden outbuilding with two rows of potting wheels along its length. The room is silent, save for the whirring of wheels. Four Japanese apprentices look up and nod. Shafts of winter sunlight make patterns on the floorboards. Plank shelves line the room, holding bowls and cups set to dry. This is where we will spend the next two days.

After I place a handful of soft, wet clay on its surface, I use my foot to push the wheel. I try to mould the clay between my hands, but I've got the wheel spinning too fast. The clay spirals up into a cone and teeters. I wrestle with clump after clump until each one falls.

Zazie has her head down in concentration. Beside her are several well-formed cups and bowls. The day lengthens, my back aches and my neck muscles are knotted. At tea break, I stand and stretch, my pride a little injured by the misshapen items I've placed on the drying shelf.

I take another clump of clay and place it on my wheel, shut my eyes and take a deep breath. The hum of the wheels is becoming hypnotic, vibrating like the chanting of monks. Then I find the moment. The weight of the clay finds its centre, spinning in perfect symmetry. My fingers become deft, letting the clay guide them. I push in and down to hollow out the centre, and a tea bowl emerges in my hands. I take a knife and carefully cut underneath, wipe my brow with the back of my sleeve, and gingerly lift the bowl from the wheel.

Late the next afternoon, everyone stops working and bows when Nakano *sensei* enters the studio. He examines the cups and bowls lining the planks, stopping here and there to pick up one. He speaks to each apprentice.

He turns to Zazie's pieces and compliments her. "*Anata wa jouzu*. You are skillful."

She flushes, thanks him and bows.

It's my turn. He picks up the tea bowl and turns it slowly in his hand. I wait, eager for him to acknowledge it. He holds it a little higher to see its full shape and then drops it on the floor.

Tears press against my orbital bone. My other pieces sit like warped reminders on the shelf, so I place them with the broken pieces of my bowl and sweep them into a pile of discarded clay.

We go to the house to say goodbye, and Nakano *sensei* surprises us again. "Please choose a piece of my work to take as parting gifts."

"*Koe desu?* Really?"

"*Yorokobimasu.* My pleasure."

I choose a tiny vase not more than three inches high. Its glaze is the colour of a pale sky, its contours seem to have been moulded to fit between the palms of my hands.

Zazie and I smile at each other, knowing we will never forget these past two days. We are leaving with the lessons of silence and concentration, and with the work of a master.

Pete walks up behind me.

"Hey."

I jump, turning red.

"How was your trip?"

I want to crow a little and tell him about the experience of throwing pots with a master. "But something awful happened," I find myself confessing.

"Nakano *sensei* smashed your bowl?"

I let out a sigh.

"That means you made something worthy."

"Then why would he destroy it?"

"By smashing the tea bowl, he was telling you to reach higher, to smash your ego, not to let it get in your way."

Trust Pete to teach me the lesson of pride.

× × ×

Mrs. Williams peers over her glasses, demanding to know whom I've been with.

"No one," I lie, hoping Celia and Brenda were able to get back to our rooms before me.

"I'm very disappointed," she says, and calls her husband. "Mr. Williams!"

As usual he seems at a loss. I feel sorry for him; it must be a trial living with his wife—and the raging estrogen of forty teenage girls.

"You're not allowed to leave campus for a week," he mutters with a quick, almost apologetic look. I trudge up to my room and find Celia under the covers with her clothes on.

"Whew, that was close," she says.

"I stayed another few minutes with Gregg. I should've left when you did. I'm grounded."

"Too bad. Tomorrow we're going to the new Fonda movie."

The next day is Saturday. It's a gloomy day, the sky threatening rain. The halls of the dorm are deserted, and the weekend lies long and boring ahead of me. I put Crosby, Stills & Nash on the turntable, place the needle on a groove and turn up the volume when "Wooden Ships" begins to play.

The song has come to define my longing for Pete. I imagine he will hear it and be drawn to my siren call.

I look out the window and my heart explodes. Is that him standing there?

"What are you doing here?"

Pete is outside the cafeteria building. "I felt like going up to the graveyard. Want to come?"

I follow him up the trail next to the creek, ducking under the branches he holds for me, until we reach the terrace overlooking the dam.

"I used to come here to escape from the dorm," he says, leaning against a tree. His eyes are moss green in the cloudy light. The creek water flows over stone, soothing the edges of my nerves. "This is my place to think."

Picking up a broken branch, I make scratches in the dirt. "I'm grounded for a week."

"Gregg told me."

His cowboy boots are scuffed, dangling at the end of his long, long legs.

"Tell me something," he says, making me look up. "I don't know much about you." The sun begins to break through the clouds, and just like that the threat of rain has ended. We talk for hours, with the mountain ridge all to ourselves.

Since that day at the graveyard, Pete and I have become easier together. We seem to bump into each other all the time. The news is filled with the "Peace with Honor" treaty to end the war in Vietnam, being negotiated in Paris, but paranoia remains. Pete's birthday, March 6, was the date of last year's draft lottery; every male eighteen years or older, born on that date, was automatically called up.

"Seriously? March 6?" If he were a year older, he might be fighting in Vietnam.

"Yeah. When I saw that, I went out and got dead drunk with Eddie."

"Would you have gone?"

"I don't know. My brother volunteered, which turned out to be smart, because he was assigned to an intelligence unit in Tokyo and gets his college paid for. Still . . ."

We let the awful thought hang in the air.

Someone is blasting music from a dorm window. In the harbour an American aircraft carrier has appeared overnight. Big things are happening, colliding, coalescing: revolutions, wars, female liberation. I sneak a sideways look at Pete. His cheekbones are cast in sharp relief and he's grown his sideburns long. I wonder if things are developing between him and Brenda, but I'm too proud to ask. Instead, I ask if he's seen the pictures from Wounded Knee, the standoff that's building in Nebraska.

There are only three months left of school. Everyone seems busy with college applications and SAT scores and talk of moving on. I've been spending a lot of time with Pete. He hasn't made a move on Brenda, and his feelings are hard to read. Mine are close to exploding. The weather is surprisingly hot for April, sticky and intense, matching my mood. After class I find him sitting near the fence, overlooking the academic field. I sit down, interrupting his solitude, and start talking about something or another. He is unusually noncommunicative.

I pick at him, spoiling for a fight. "You aren't even listening. I don't know what you are thinking." And then it bursts out: "What do you think of me?"

He points up at the sky. I catch a glimpse of a white bird ascending, following its sweep and rise.

"You are up there, above everything," he says.

His lips are on mine before I realize what is happening. I feel the probing of his tongue, its taste of *mikan* and tobacco. He kisses me so deep I want to cry.

His hands are in my hair, pulling me closer, until there's no space in between.

Dazed, we finally break apart.

"How long—?" I want to know.

He puts his fingers to my lips. "Shh, don't speak." And then he kisses me again.

Square white boards with yellow water stains still line the bedroom ceiling. Celia is a lump under her covers. Our room is in its usual disarray of books and clothes and albums, but nothing feels the same. I look at the clock: five a.m. Too early to get up. I've hardly slept, floating all night in a dreamlike state, reliving every detail of the evening before.

After the kiss, I stayed in his arms until it was time to sign in to the dorm. We said goodnight, but then he turned as he was leaving. He didn't ask me out on a date. He did not say the expected things.

"I want to make love to you."

My face burned, words caught in my throat. "Me too," I managed to whisper.

The first day of school, I saw him kissing a girl. I'd stopped in my tracks, wishing I were her. Now I am the girl.

× × ×

Dear Shelley,
I dreamt I was lying with my head in a woman's lap, and she was stroking my face, talking softly. I was completely connected to the woman, a deep, epical, long-abiding love rooted in years and years of history. I just sank, sank into that sensation of rightness in my world, enfolded in love, as if dying. You were the woman in my dream; who else? I remember the exact shape of your hands and fingers from when we were together. I remember holding your hand, and the feeling of you tucked under my arm. Based on some other dreams I've had, I can also add most emphatically that it was not metaphorical.

First Light

PETE IS THERE on the mountain at dawn, waiting.

"You're here early."

"I went up to the dam and watched the sun rise."

I bury my face in his neck where it meets his shoulder, as though I'm a homing bird that knows this exact place, as though we've been together for a thousand years. Just like that, we have become *us*.

After class I know where to find him. I follow the strains of his harmonica up past the stream. He is almost camouflaged, his army jacket merging with the ferns, dried pine needles and moss, his hazel eyes reflecting the natural elements. He reaches for my hand to pull me down.

The air is thick and pungent with the scent of white plum blossoms that have scattered after a few days of rain. We nestle in our private world, hidden from our classmates, though some already know.

Zazie had looked a little confused the night I curled up

on her sofa and made my confession. She shook her head slowly as if she was missing something.

I said, "Are you upset I never told you?"

"No."

"Then why are you shaking your head?"

"I thought you were already lovers."

Gregg had snorted with laughter.

Mary crushed me in a bear hug. "Pete's been acting so weird lately, I figured it must be you."

Yvonne said, "Cool."

Celia had practically pounced when I returned to our room, flushed from the kiss. "Why are your clothes rumpled?"

I smoothed down my shirt.

"Tell me!"

"I love Pete." There it was, the simple truth.

She shrieked, demanding details, recounting all the times I had put him down.

"Stop!" I begged, laughing. Then I got serious. "It's about Brenda—"

But Celia pre-empted me. "Brenda's a guy magnet. Don't worry, she'll get over it."

Brenda avoided me for a few days, but late one night we sat on the floor in her room and had a heart-to-heart. She told me she was still pining for her old boyfriend, that Pete was a fleeting crush. I wanted to believe her. I apologized for keeping my feelings secret for so long.

× × ×

After confiding in our closest friends, it's good to escape to our private place and be alone. Pete gently pushes me back until I am lying on the ground. He reaches under my shirt to unclasp my bra. His fingers know where to touch, and I shudder. Now he is on top of me, kissing me deeper, pressing me hard through his jeans. In a turmoil of wanting, he whispers, "We have to stop . . . before I can't stop."

We have decided to make it special. We have agreed to wait.

Floating just above and just beyond all I have known, I exist in a universe where Pete is my North Star. He takes my hand and leads. We go to his favourite cafés and bars, his favourite vendors of baked yams and barbecued squid.

"*Oishii ne?*" Yes. Delicious.

Let It Be has arrived in Japan, like most films and albums, long after its original release date and is playing at the Kokusai Plaza Theatre. We watch the film with subtitles. The Beatles' last recording sessions. Yoko and John hold hands in the listening booth. Pete is holding mine. We watch the most famous band in the world, the soundtrack of our youth, breaking up as though in real time—but it's already happened. Pete's thigh brushes against mine.

On the streets outside, shop signs are peppered with mangled sixties slang. Everything seems out of time. We point them out, laughing at "I Dig U Apple" at the entrance to a café, and "Groove Pie" over the door of a pizza place.

At Pete's favourite coffee shop we slide in to a table and the owner comes over to say hi. They shoot the breeze in Japanese while I listen to Janis Joplin's *Pearl.*

"Great singer, but the Holding Company sucks." Pete finishes his conversation with his friend by talking about Janis's band.

"He's a great musician," Pete says about the café owner, who has left us. Then he switches topics. "Another one came to talk to me today." He's referring to the CIA recruitment types who regularly scout our campus. Easy to spot, they are usually Caucasian men with bad haircuts, wearing business suits.

"What did he say?"

"Free tuition wherever I want to go to college, and then we'll see."

"What did you say?"

He raises an eyebrow and gives me the look that says *I can't believe you're asking.* Like a set of lacquer nesting boxes, he opens up, layer by layer, sharing his concerns, doubts and decisions about the future. He's been accepted by top universities and has chosen the University of Michigan, in Ann Arbor, to be close to me. I think about how much he will miss this place. How he told me he always dreams in Japanese. I am beginning to experience disorientation, as though this time is already a memory and I'm not ready to move on.

"Maybe we should stay, spend another year? We could find a place and I'll learn the language."

He considers for a moment. "No, I'm ready to go. Don't

worry, we won't be apart for long." He gives me one of his lazy, crazy smiles. I'm caught off guard by his beauty.

Walking over raked pebbles that make circles and patterns on the ground, we follow the path of devotees through the vermilion gate to the temple. Pete stops to look at the reflection of trees wavering in a pond. He teaches me to take a moment. A scent of burning aloeswood wafting from the altar, the quiet of the hallowed space reverberating like an incantation. Pete teaches me silence, too.

He shows me rocks and trees that are believed to be inhabited by *nami*, spirits. He is my fixed point, my *sensei*.

"Did you know *renkon*, lotus root, is considered an aphrodisiac?"

"Really?"

"Ginger too."

"How do you know that?"

"I just do."

He lays his head in my lap and looks at the sky. I stroke his sideburns and his brows, place the palms of my hands against the mound of his cheekbones, brush the soft, full centre of his bottom lip, trace the edges of his mouth. I want to explore every surface, to memorize him.

"You don't blush anymore," he teases.

"Thank god."

"Actually, I kind of miss it."

× × ×

> Dear Shelley;
> You used to hold my arm with both of your hands
> and lean your head into my shoulder when we were
> walking really slowly, as if afraid of losing that
> physical contact. God, I loved that, and it felt as
> if we were walking through an old French film.
> I remember walking down Sanchikatan (remember?)
> after a film, and I said something about your French
> admirer that made you stop, laugh and then blush.
> You were bewitching, you know that? The jeans
> and flannel shirt live in my memory, but I also
> remember every curve inside your clothes, and
> our first time . . .

The school year is ending and that means an end to our time in Japan, just when we have finally come together.

Pete brings it up first. He does it in his usual grown-up way. "Are you on the pill?"

"No . . ."

His expression changes as a new idea takes hold. "You're a virgin."

I nod, embarrassed but not ashamed.

He pulls me close and then very calmly explains how the pill works, the gaps in the days, the cycle. "I think you should start it soon."

Pete and I enter the hotel ballroom. The sign says "Congratulations, Graduates! Canadian Academy Class of 73." I'm wearing a backless black dress, a dark slash among all the pastel and lace. Pete is wearing a green corduroy jacket and a tie.

When he pulls me onto the dance floor, the room disappears. We sway together, naked with longing.

Dear Shelley,
The night of graduation you were drop-dead beautiful in a black dress, a lot of skin and eyes. Throughout dinner all I could think of was that I wanted to rip that dress off, set fire to every inch of your body with my lips and then make love to you, over and over. That was a rough night.

Eddie stopped by with some friends to say hello, and he told me in Japanese that we looked really good together, and good luck. He had an unusually sincere look in his eyes, and an even more sober tone, and the slightly formal language he used was to let me know it was a "moment." It was probably one of the nicest things anyone said to me in those last days.

Dear Daniel,
I woke up and looked at the alarm clock. It was six a.m. I lay there and then started drifting. I was lying next to you and you began to touch me and my body started to tremble. I began to touch you. Every part of me was on edge. I had all these sensations and I wanted to kiss you with such deep longing that it hurt. I wanted to drink you in. It was very erotic, but also very incomplete.

I got up. I was tired but not tired. I had so much energy. I felt so alive.

My Dearest Shelley,
I almost have your last letter memorized by now, but I think I could read it a hundred more times and get just as aroused and dizzy on every reading. If you can hear that roaring sound, that's the sound of the 10,000 butterflies in my belly flapping their wings, making me feel like a teenager.

Shelley, we did it again, your email came just as I finished this last bit. We were talking about exactly the same thing. I love what you wrote, it's like having you touch me, and I'm glad I'm in your blood, I want to be there always.

Wildflower

THE WIND FREEZES a band across my forehead. I nestle the earphones connected to Daniel's iPod into place, letting Sheryl Crow's "Wildflower" pace my footfalls. It's a song about a lover showing up when beauty has lost its way.

Mono no aware, fleeting love.

It has been seven months since Daniel died. The park is almost empty; people are elsewhere, busy with their lives. I put one boot in front of the other, punching through layers of frozen snow and ice. The sky is leaden, and the frozen cityscape is an abstract in black and white. If I were filming this scene, I would not be in it—I have fallen out of the present, pulled backwards in time, like succumbing to an addictive drug.

Hair whips around my face. Pete and I are on the deck of the overnight ferry, crossing over to the island of Shikoku in the south. He has his arm around my shoulder and pulls me closer as the harbour recedes. The sun is about to dip beneath the waves and disappear.

"I'm going to show you everything," he says.

I am surfacing with the evening air, emerging from the last days of school, from the womb of childhood. I am ready to know him as a lover. From the first look this has been inevitable.

We will spend our last ten days in Japan together, alone. He is taking me to Kochi, where two rivers meet the sea.

He rubs my bottom lip with his thumb. I feel it pulse and swell. Eyes shut now, tasting saltwater spray with each other's tongue. The smell of ship oil mingles with the scent of his sweet breath. He presses in hard to let me feel him. There is no turning back, no return to the shore.

A fellow traveller passes by. "*Sumimasen*, excuse me."

Startled, we smile. "*Gomen nasai*," Pete says. Sorry.

I smooth down my clothes and gaze up at the sky. I can make out Orion's Belt and the Big Dipper and a blur of distant galaxies. The quarter-moon shines a cone of light onto the black waves. The traveller walks on, leaving us to ourselves: young lovers from some foreign land crossing the Inland Sea.

Pete speaks with the proprietor, a woman with a kindly face. She seems to be telling him a story while we check in.

"Name?"

"Mr. and Mrs. Oscar Wilde."

"*Wa-ri-du, desuka?*"

"*Hai, so desu.*" Pete and I avoid eye contact lest we burst out laughing.

Twin beds take up most of the Western-style room. We try to push them together but they are bolted to the floor. This will be our first night alone together, but something is amiss. It feels formal, adult. Suddenly it all feels too planned.

Pete lights a joint. "I thought this would relax us."

He leads me to one of the beds and we sit and have a toke. I'm feeling anxious. I wish we were outside in beauty, letting our natural pull to each other find its way, not in this boxed-in room.

He says, "I'll be back in a minute," and goes into the bathroom.

Now he is standing naked and fully aroused before me. My breath catches. I haven't seen a man this way before.

I let him undress me, but I'm tense, disconnected. Still, I open my arms, falling into the role of adult lover the way I've imagined.

The weed has me paranoid. The room seems to be spinning.

He moves on top. It feels like his weight is crushing me. It feels like he will split me open. Fear replaces desire, and I panic. "No! I'm sorry, I can't."

"It's okay," he says, moving to the other bed.

"Pete, I'm sorry," I whisper sometime in the night.

He doesn't answer, either asleep or pretending to be. My eyes leak silent tears.

In the morning, the ugly room is flooded with blinding light. When I open my eyes, Pete is already dressed. We pay for our room and grab our backpacks. I try to put the night out of my mind, to push the darkness away. When we walk outside, Pete doesn't reach for my hand, stuffing his in his pockets.

Kochi sits hot and humid on the edge of Urado Bay. A tropical bank of green covers one hillside; in the other direction are mountains. At the heart of the city is Kochi Castle. A sign says it was built by a shogun in 1600.

Pete is walking ahead on the path up to its ramparts where he played as a boy. He'd been excited to show it to me, but now I'm feeling excluded. He is distant, lost in his childhood memories, or maybe just distant from me.

His primary school, now shuttered and closed for the summer, is a series of low buildings with classrooms. This is where he made his first friends, learned his first kanji, where he was fully accepted as a Japanese schoolboy. He is silent, looking through the classroom windows into another time.

Outside his childhood home there's a garden wall, through which we can make out roses and wisteria.

"My father planted and replanted after each typhoon." He tells me this and a few other things, but mostly he's quiet. In the late afternoon we walk on the beach where the river and ocean meet, picking up river stones. A wall has grown up between us.

"About last night . . ." I say.

"Don't worry."

"You're angry."

"No, I'm not."

The sunlight dances on the waves; our dark shadows move separately across the sand.

× × ×

Alone in the winter park, "Wildflower" is still playing, the wistful lyrics matching my memory. A bird's nest high up in a leafless tree commands my eyes. My mind is seeking something to hold on to.

I stomp my boots to bring blood to my toes, the reptilian brain directing my body to stay warm, to survive. But what if I can't? I want to leave this frozen place, but I don't want to go home. What can I find to ease the crushing weight on my chest? I don't know how to recover from this.

A fierce gust rips the breath from my lungs, rattling the bare branches, which crack and moan.

Pete and I travelled in silence. Not a calm quiet, when you can hear the rustling of trees. Not the quiet of pilgrimage. This is something else. This silence screams at me.

We are now upstream from Kochi in Nakamura, on the Shimanto River. There is a tiny beach of river stone outside the ryokan where Pete is checking us in. The innkeeper asks if I'd like to take a bath. Yes.

I enter the women's *ofuro*, dip my washcloth into a wooden bucket of soapy water and begin to wash away the past twenty-four hours. Climb into the steaming bath and let tension melt in the scalding water, until body and mind are one.

Returning to our room, I notice the housekeeper has unrolled the futon mattress on the floor and laid out cotton kimonos. Shoji doors are open to the river.

Pete is sitting cross-legged, sipping a cup of tea. I join him but we find no words to speak. A shaft of moonlight forms a slash across our mattress and onto the tatami floor.

We prepare for bed.

In the dark he appears like a ridge, his back to me.

"Please, don't turn away." I am on my side, facing him. I stroke his hair until he turns towards me. "Thank you for showing me your childhood today. Thank you for understanding."

He leans over and kisses my throat. Slips the kimono from my shoulder and kisses me there.

His mouth is hot and wet on my nipple. His head is in my hands. Desire mounting, we move closer still, until there's no moonlight between us. I untie the belt of his kimono and reach to touch him there for the first time, feeling satin skin stretched over his hardness.

He moves down between my legs, taking his time, tongue turning my insides to liquid fire. Then he is up and over me, saying, "I'm sorry, this will hurt."

I cry out his name, whisper it, moan it over and over until he owns me, until I own him, and every part of us is wide open.

× × ×

Dear Shelley,

I will never, ever forget having been your first.

I remember every moment. Franco Zeffirelli would
have filmed our movie, and Michel Legrand would

> have written the score. As for the players, no direction was needed. It was incredibly romantic.
>
> I remember looking at your face early in the morning as you slept, knowing we would soon part, wondering where you were headed, and thinking that time was racing, racing, not enough time for you and me, not enough time to know all I wanted to know. In those early morning hours, I made several promises to myself about how I would treat the times to come; some which I kept, others failed the test of time.

Filters of sunlight on tatami. Shoji screen open to the river. I rub my eyes. He is leaning against the window, silhouetted by dawn's early light. Beautiful boy.

Wrapping the yukata around me, I prop myself up on one arm. "You are awake?"

A shy smile. "Yes."

"Couldn't sleep?"

"Been sitting here thinking."

I open my arms to him. Come inside.

I stumble, slipping on a bit of black ice hidden beneath the powder of snow. Someone walks past, talking loudly into a smartphone, stressed voice rising louder, something about a crucial deadline. The wind whips and stings.

The person on deadline rushes ahead towards Queen Street, leaving the park to me again. The faint circle of a pale winter sun briefly lights the sky.

The song stops when I finally turn back to go home. A canvas bleached of colour; a bed track stripped of sound.

Replay. Da capo.

Pete and I spend our days exploring. Hiking through ancient cedar groves, along mountain and coastal paths overlooking endless beautiful shorelines, following the route of the eighty-eight temple pilgrimage. *Henros*, pilgrims dressed in white, appear here and there along mostly deserted paths. We climb the hundreds of stone steps to ancient temples, following the path of the Buddhist monk Kukai, the path of awakening. Pete shows me where the wildflowers grow.

Our silences are now filled with awe. At temple gates we bow low, rinse our hands and sip water to cleanse our mouths, light incense inside the ancient halls, and leave coins with our names and wishes. Bells toll. Mantras are chanted.

We rarely let go of each other's hand. We snack on delicious yuzu, tasting the tang of citrus on our tongues. In the evenings we feast on soba noodles, sit outside and look at the moon, return to our room to make love.

Wandering through hidden places, the crevices and secrets, the scars and stories our bodies hold. I want to breathe the same breath as Pete. I want to stay lost in him.

When it's time to leave, we take a train bound for Hiroshima. At a station along the way we are taken by surprise when our classmates Mark and Ellen jump aboard.

"Smile." Mark captures us with his lens.

On our last night in Japan, I sit on a single bed, my suitcase packed. All my other belongings have already been shipped to Canada.

Pete knocks quietly, lets himself in. We are back in Kobe, at his parents'. It feels so strange. After our trip alone together, we are children again in his parents' home, where I am staying in the guest room.

Pete sits beside me and we stare at each other, memorizing what we've already memorized. "Your eyes have amber in them," he says.

"They're brown."

"No, they have flecks of gold." He brushes my bottom lip with his finger. "And this freckle is a beauty mark." He covers the mark with his lips.

We linger as long as we can before he says goodnight and retreats to his room.

In the morning, his father drives us to Osaka Airport. Pete is catching a flight to Bangkok to begin his journey to the States, travelling through Asia and Europe until summer's end. I am returning to Beijing.

His plane leaves first. We cling together until the last boarding call, and then he hands me a letter and disappears through the gate.

From the oval plane window, I watch the islands of Japan recede beneath the clouds, already becoming a memory. I've said goodbye to my friends and teachers. I've said goodbye to the view from the ridge. I've said goodbye to Pete. I am leaving something behind, something of youth that defies definition, something impossible to repeat.

I unfold his letter.

Dear Shelley,

By now you are on the plane. And I am on mine.

You must excuse me while I write down all the things that actually go without saying. There was a joy in waking up to go to school to see you. No one has ever given me more and never before have I been more able to receive. You helped me feel so much in love. I feel no regrets or remorse about our relationship starting when it did. Whether being away from each other will be good for us or not, I feel that I've accepted it, and hope that fate will be kind. There are so many possibilities that I refuse to ignore, for us.

I've thought and appreciated ALL; all that we've had together, and just in case I never told you, I've never been able to share so much with someone before in all my life(s)? (That I can recall—assuming that we have never met before.)

I LOVE YOU.

Pete

A dog barks, a cyclist whizzes past on the icy pathway.

"Wildflower" has ended. I look down at the iPod and for the first time I notice that it says "Daniel Pete"—Peterson being too long for the screen. Daniel. Pete.

My eyelashes freeze with tears. Daylight is fading fast. I head home thinking about the choices we make, thinking about life's fragility.

"Nothing is going to come between us again," I remember I told him on the phone the night before I flew to see him again in 2002. I was flying blind and taking a leap, but I put my faith in a girl of seventeen, the one who knew her heart.

In Between

NINE MONTHS HAVE passed. A cluster of hyacinths has pushed through the soil in his garden to bloom on his birthday, March 6. He was a Pisces, emotionally sensitive and easily hurt. A dreamer.

They say it takes time, but I'm still in a place where the chasm keeps growing, bigger than I can hold. I'm unable to hear his voice today; there's just a cavern of silence. So I pick at the scabs, churning up regrets that death makes permanent, mistakes that can never be unwritten.

I randomly select an old journal from my shelf, a school exercise book covered with a Japanese paper. Inscribed in ink in my handwriting, the label reads "Srinagar." I'm in Kashmir.

Houseboat, Dal Lake, August 1973. Chanting from the mosque fills the mountain air. The canals of green floating gardens, tumbledown water houses, roosters, chickens, the dipping of oars across the lake.

Filling my notebook with imaginings, quotations of poetry and sketches of the lotus flowers that grow in the lake around our houseboat, I look up and observe their stems rising ridiculously high from roots hidden in the mud, a profundity of pink blooms dotting the azure water.

And then, suddenly I'm filled with the same old longing, longing, longing. It hits me full force. I want to be with him now.

My mom and I are staying on an old British houseboat on Dal Lake in Srinagar. From our floating veranda is the vista that inspired the fictional Shangri-La. But I'm only half here. I copy a paragraph from Pete's last letter from Bangkok into my notebook.

> ***Dear Shelley,***
>
> ***It rained on the way back; the countryside suddenly became a beautiful dark green and the wind came to life, pushing the palm trees back and forth. It was all a very pretty sight. It seemed ageless and cyclic—like order in chaos whenever I see a storm.***

I miss him so much it hurts.

I jot down observations of this land nestled in the Himalayas: the mystics and Sufis, Muslim women covered in black, hippies with backpacks wearing batik cloth, and relics of the Raj that are everywhere, including the fine bone china and musty books that line the carved bookshelves in our floating living room. We fall asleep listening to rock music coming from the ongoing party on the boat next to ours, and wake to the sound of lapping water and the call to prayer.

This trip is my eighteenth-birthday present: a surprise exotic trek back to Canada with my mom. My dad has stayed on in Beijing to help his successor at the Canadian embassy before he flies home with my brother and sister. Vendors row up in shikaras laden with treasures: embroidered shawls, topaz and lapis. I look at my mom—she is very beautiful, only thirty-five years old. She barters for gems with a man named Ali. I choose a carved Krishna that fits in the palm of my hand. We laugh and act like sisters, but occasionally some friction reminds me that I am still her child.

"Why don't you wear your glasses? You can't see a thing. Don't be vain!"

"I can see."

She's right. The blue and pink of lake and lotus are a blurred Impressionist painting, but I stubbornly leave my glasses in their case. I'm close to my mom and can tell her things, but I haven't really spoken of Pete. When it comes to him, I hoard my privacy. My parents do not know the depth of us.

I imagine his hands on my body. Eyes shut, smiling into the sun, an unbidden memory floats in.

The setting is a path to a Shinto shrine. We stop just outside the gate to sip water to purify our souls.

"What if I'm pregnant?"

He places the wooden dipper back on the edge of the stone basin.

"But you're on the pill."

"I know, but . . ."

I don't tell him that I got a month's supply from a girlfriend the day before we left Kobe and started taking the pills partway through my cycle. I know that's not how they are supposed to work, and now I'm a little worried.

He puts his arm around me and kisses the top of my head. We reach the entrance, and he purchases an *omikuji* fortune, unfolding the accordion of paper.

"What does it say?"

"'You will meet the path you are destined for.'"

After a few days the cramps start, blood washing away the uncertainty. I rush out of the bathroom to tell Pete. We are at Mary's house in Hiroshima, our last stop before returning to Kobe. I am moody, feeling strange. Mary's parents are away and her friends crowd the living room. Everyone is listening to music; everyone is speaking in Japanese. I want to share my news with Pete. I want him to myself.

I feel a tinge of disappointment mingled with relief. *Maybe it's because our time is coming to an end*, I think, inserting myself next to him and resting my head on his shoulder. Or maybe it's history. After all, my mom had me at seventeen.

·

I look up from my notebook; my mother is dressed and ready to go. On a bus heading up Shankaracharya Hill, the sky darkens. After weeks of blue skies, a storm is moving in. Tourists clamber off the bus, heads bowed against the wind, and walk to Shiva's temple. Shiva is the creator and protector of the universe, the guide says. He is also the destroyer. The Lord of the Universe sits in lotus position in the dark interior.

He is white except for his neck, which is blue and circled by a serpent.

"White because he is covered in the ashes of corpses," the guide tells us. A clap of thunder breaks in the distance. "The blue on his neck is from venom."

Fat drops of rain hit the roof. The skies open up and it pours.

I think of Pete on a beach somewhere, enjoying his travels. Unbidden, doubt poisons my mood.

We are back home in Toronto. It's September 1973, just in time for school to begin. Our house is in shambles. The renters, a family who had promised to care for our home and look after our dog, had abandoned the premises mid-year and sublet it to five chefs, who turned it into a party house.

In the living room my mom discovers that her prized coffee table with the marble top has been cracked down the middle. The room we kept locked, a small bedroom in the basement filled with family treasures, old art projects, report cards and photo albums, has been busted into, and our things lie trampled on the floor. Our dog, Scotty, has taken up residence with a neighbour.

Word is out that we've returned. The doorbell keeps ringing, people keep arriving, and my Toronto friends collect in gangs on our porch. They look bemused at my ankle-length embroidered dress from a market in Istanbul, suddenly out of place amidst their shorts and T-shirts.

I'm happy to see them but feel dislocated, out of step with

their lives. They regale me with news: who is seeing whom, which couple has broken up, who has come out of the closet. I've brought gifts, old silk kimonos from the Kyoto market and other items I want to give them during quiet reconnections, and I have stories to share. But things are constantly frantic.

My father is in a foul mood, missing his diplomatic role in one of the world's most exciting posts, returning to the world of petty university politics. My mom has gone back to her job as a social worker, coming home after work and putting dinner on the table. In Beijing she had a cook and a housemaid and now she is both again. She expects me to help, and I do, but I want to slink off and be alone. I feel like a fifth wheel in my nuclear family; during their intense year in Beijing they have coalesced as a gang of four.

I've been accepted into Theatre Arts at York University, what I've wanted so badly, but getting a placement in the performance stream is competitive, and the audition is in one week's time.

The phone rings. "It's for you." My dad gives me a look as he hands over the receiver.

"Shelley!" Pete's voice breaks up with static, punching through from another reality. "I'm in Ann Arbor. I'm coming to Toronto."

"Oh, wow." I pause, appalled at the timing. I haven't chosen a scene for my audition; I've barely unpacked. "Pete, it's not really a good time. Could we wait until things settle a little? When do your classes start?"

My mom is calling me to set the table. I miss what he says next. "Pardon?"

"I'll be there tomorrow."

And there he is, striding towards me at the Greyhound bus station. I catch my breath in dismay, seeing him through the eyes of my parents. Even to me he has changed. His hair hangs well past his shoulders; a shark's tooth dangles from one ear. He's wearing more silver on his fingers, his nails are dirty and his clothes reek of cigarettes. He's the wayfarer we passed on the hippie trail in India, the guy who played music for change on the streets of Amsterdam. It's been only two and a half months since we parted, but he looks years older.

He puts down his guitar case and swings me in his arms, and for a moment it is *us* again. I feel the rough stubble on his chin when he kisses me. But I'm conflicted. Embarrassed and confused. Not ready to take him home.

Instead I take him to High Park, near my house. I need a bridge between worlds. Sitting cross-legged on the grass, he tells me about the beach he slept on in Corfu, where Swedish girls kept trying to seduce him, and about busking on the streets of Rotterdam. I feel like I'm listening to a stranger.

When he tries to make out, I become shy. "Pete, someone will see us."

He persists until I push him away. "Seriously," I say.

He lights a cigarette. I can't put a finger on my emotions. Soon it will be dinner time—I'd better get this over with. "Let's go meet my family."

When we come in the door, I want to protect Pete from the way they look at him. I want to protect them from him, too. My perfect, too-young family isn't ready for another male adult.

My father tells Pete he is welcome to sleep in the basement—three flights from my bedroom.

I am embarrassed by my surroundings: so normal, so middle-class, so decidedly unexotic. The doorbell keeps ringing; more friends are standing on the porch. Pete retreats to the basement. I hear him strumming his guitar.

We have no place to be alone, but when we are alone, I feel exposed. A distance has crept in somewhere between Beijing and Bangkok, or betweeen Istanbul and Greece, where Pete smoked dope and warded off women. "I was faithful to you," he says, but his reference to sex just embarrasses me.

I sequester myself in my bedroom in the attic of our house to practise for my audition. When I come back downstairs, my dad is grilling Pete in the living room.

"Why in the world would you study classical Chinese at university? What good will that do you?" he wants to know.

"Bill!" says my mom in her fun-but-warning tone. "Leave the poor guy alone." She turns to Pete. "It's nice to have you here. Shelley really missed you."

"Do you want to meet my friends?" I ask after dinner. "There's a party tonight."

"I'd rather just hang out with you."

"Pete, I haven't seen them in a year and a half. If it's okay with you, I'm going."

Later, when we return from the party he reluctantly went to, he says, "You're different here."

I can't admit that he makes me feel embarrassed by my Toronto friends, who next to him seem so parochial. "No, I'm not." I storm up to my bedroom.

Each day the separation grows. Words that once flowed like an endless tide have become scarce—stuck, harsh, short, harder and harder to say. We no longer look directly at each other. Instead we exchange sideways glances, heads hung low, skulking around the fridge at night.

"Would you like something to drink?" We have become polite.

A crate arrives and sits in the driveway. It's so large it looks like someone could live in it.

"Must be a mistake," my father tells the delivery guys.

"Nope, says right here: Saywell. From Japan."

I had left a trunk at Yvonne's house in Kobe when I cleared out of the dorm and took off to travel with Pete. Yvonne, who was headed for Ottawa, offered to help with the shipping.

"You can add a few things of your own," I said, to thank her for her many kindnesses to me. Half of her Kobe house seems to be in the crate: boxes and boxes of books, pottery and clothes, a wooden *tansu* chest and an enormous hibachi.

My dad won't look at me. "This is an abuse of government funding," he snaps. "It must have cost a bloody fortune."

The next day Yvonne rolls in from Ottawa towing a U-Haul, with a much older guy, her new boyfriend. She's wearing a long, flowing dress.

I tell her, "Before we go into the house, I should warn you, my dad is furious about the shipment. And I don't think he's too happy about Pete being here either."

Pete is very happy to see her. He and Yvonne's boyfriend escape to the park to smoke dope.

A little later my uncle and cousins arrive for yet another reunion. By the time Pete and her boyfriend return, totally wasted, Yvonne is holding court with stories of growing up in Japan, and there are twenty people in our living room.

My mom asks Pete if he would mind helping her clear the basement. She talks to him, asks him about his parents and China. She is trying to make him feel at home, trying to help me out. My brother shows him some of his drawings. But nothing seems to bridge the gap between Pete and me. Our silences have turned sullen.

"He's really cute," Trish, now eleven, says to comfort me.

My mom nods. "Classically handsome."

I ask her, "Could you tell Dad to back off?"

"I'll try." But we both know my dad is not really the problem.

I can't focus on the audition. I'm feeling culture shock, and something more. I don't know how to be both a girl and a woman in the house of my childhood. I don't know how to be with Pete.

One night, I find a letter/poem on my bed.

Shelley,

I write, knowing there's one person in this world that is impossible to leave.

Hoping a back will turn, but knowing a futile hope when an end becomes almost real.

A half-hearted ciao, *a final intense wish, and sudden loneliness.*

Good night? A reunion is often shy
But feel the fear grow.
The mortar sets, the bricks multiply.
But lovers break them down. My love lives.

I love you.
Pete

All these years later, I wonder. Why didn't I sneak downstairs in the middle of the night and climb into his bed? Or take him somewhere, like the park, and kiss him over and over.

Why was I so embarrassed? Why was I so proud? Why did I fixate on "*ciao*" and "mortar sets" and not his words about love? I still have the letter. I found it tucked in the back of a journal, its creases made permanent with time. I read it so differently now.

Was it fear that our love was too big for my small world? Was it only pride? Today, on his birthday, I am wishing I could have protected him from all the pain to come. Especially the pain I caused.

"I'm leaving."

I can barely look him in the eye, feeling a mixture of anger at myself and relief that he's departing early. He had planned to stay for a week, but I don't offer a protest, don't even apologize.

"Don't you want to go in with him, honey?" my mom asks while I sit sullen in the backseat of her car outside the Greyhound station, where we've dropped him.

"No. Please, just drive." I want the guilt and embarrassment of this week to end. I want to go home and stick my head under the pillow. But when I do, all I can see is Pete walking away, tall and lanky, with his guitar case in his hand.

Of course I mess up the audition. I know it the moment I enter the room.

York University campus feels like an outpost on the moon. Concrete buildings spread across a windswept campus; massive lecture halls make us all anonymous. It takes an hour and a half to commute each way by subway and bus. I sit alone in a bleak mental landscape. I miss Japan. I miss my friends. Most of all, I miss Pete.

Two months go by. Between classes, I go to the cafeteria to meet a new friend, a mature student in his thirties. He's trying to rewrite his life and is, in my view, wise. He has earned his opinions.

I tell him about Pete. "Love like that doesn't come around twice," he warns. "Listen to me, I'm living proof. Get on a damn bus and go see him."

Instead I write Pete a letter. I suggest a visit to Ann Arbor at American Thanksgiving. I write as though nothing has happened.

An envelope addressed in his handwriting waits on the ledge over the radiator in our entrance hall, where we place keys and mittens. I race up to my bedroom, close the door, tear open the envelope. Rushing through the letter, I read his polite words. He writes about his classes, new friends and the music scene on campus. In the final paragraph he mentions a "very fine" girl he met in art class, the girl he is now with.

I light a cigarette, open a window. Holding the letter against the flame of my lighter, I set it on fire, watching it curl and burn. I think of Shiva the destroyer, covered in white, as ashes float and fall on my hands.

Months later, I write one last letter, with an apology. It comes back "return to sender"—person or address unknown.

It's midnight. At last his birthday is over. This is a year of "first" anniversaries, each a minefield. I have survived my birthday, our anniversary, Christmas and New Year's, and now his birthday. I am learning to be alone.

Still. I want to be back in the place where everything is possible. I want to feel the stubble at his throat rough against my skin. I want to feel him reaching for my hand. I want to smell him. I rush to his closet, pull out his favourite scarf and bury my face in its folds.

Back then, I should have got on a bus to Ann Arbor anyway. I should have just shown up, without warning. The new girlfriend, like the one before me in Japan, would have disappeared in the light and heat we created. All it would have taken was a twenty-five-dollar bus ticket—and an act of courage.

Pete, the student our teachers expected to excel at college, dropped out of university and returned to Japan.

Brenda was finishing her senior year at CA and asked me in a letter, "What happened to you guys? He won't even mention your name."

I abandoned my dream of a career in theatre, transferred to the University of Toronto, and took courses in Islamic, Indian and Sanskrit studies, Japanese woodblock prints and the poetry of Yeats. My new boyfriend Rob and I moved in together during my final year. We drank and smoked too much, stayed up late playing music. It was a fun and easy love and ended like it started.

"I think I'll go out to Alberta," he said, just like in the song.

"Sounds good," I answered, ready to move on. But for me, going forward meant going back. I had decided to rejoin the path I was destined for.

I would return to Japan to find Pete.

The Ride

AFTER ALL THE words written of a love never forgotten, all our email confessions and feelings renewed on the phone, after seven long months of healing on his part, Daniel said he was ready to meet. He sent me a plane ticket.

His physical transformation had astonished his friends and coworkers—everyone except his physiotherapist, Bonnie. She knew what had gotten him through the pain. The most powerful cure is love.

Since returning from Iraq, I had raced the clock; the edit needed to be fast. My distributor kept calling: German television wanted the film, so did France. More deadlines, different versions. It was only two months until the January 17 deadline, until the U.S. unleashed the threatened "shock and awe" bombing campaign on Baghdad. Now everyone wanted an inside view of Iraq. Deborah Palloway, the film's editor, had broken up with her partner and temporarily moved into my house. We worked late into the night in the makeshift edit room in my attic, sometimes in our pajamas, cataloguing footage, pulling interviews, hiring translators and typing transcripts.

Now my personal deadline was looming too. In two weeks I would fly to Utah, where Daniel was living. We were planning seven days together, after seven months of waiting. Those seven days might be heaven or they might feel like an eternity.

In the mirror I studied the years on my face. What would he see? I got my hair trimmed, had a bikini wax, and went shopping. I bought a long skirt because its silken folds felt sexy against my legs and its vintage look reminded me of the seventies, and chose a warm sweater in case it was cold in the mountains of Utah where we were planning to hole up. On impulse I bought a sweater for him too.

Our expectations had grown big and wild, harder and harder to rein in. We were practically making love on the phone. Was this a desperate attempt to regain our youth? Was I becoming a cliché? I mostly couldn't sleep. When I did, my dreams were scenes I kept rewriting. Scenes from the edit room, scenes from the past, children in peril, politicians telling lies, chemical weapons, the burdens of history, burned tanks in the desert left to rot, behemoths from the first Gulf War. Deadlines, deadlines. War, approaching. A trip somewhere. A desert of red rock. A place I didn't know. A place in the past.

Maybe love, coming around again. Maybe love. Again.

Broken

MY MOTHER HAS lost her words. She has primary progressive aphasia, a disease of the frontal lobe that causes words to jumble, disjoint and evaporate until, unbearably, they are gone. She has also lost her memory. We missed the early signs because Daniel and my brother-in-law James were diagnosed with cancer around the same time and our family was overcome by trauma. During their illnesses and after they died, she'd consoled Trish and me, telling us she "loved us to bits." Now that she can't say those words and doesn't know who we are, the burden is on us to remember.

I find it unfathomable to imagine life without words and memories, my beacons in the dark. I want to find words to give meaning to the meaningless, the ridiculous, the unforgivable, the stupid, the unfair, the cruel—all the things impossible to comprehend. Words like *dementia* or *widow* or *cancer* or *bereaved* seem too small. How can they contain the enormity of loss?

I worry someday I will lose my words too, so I say the big

words out loud. *Love. Healing. Forgiveness.* I listen to the sound they make and feel them on my tongue. When committed to paper, they appear solid and bold, even when they feel like lies. I want to have faith in their meaning. I want to believe that words can make you whole.

I was ready to meet Daniel, but I already knew the man he'd become, through his words. I had drunk them like wine, words that described what he thought and felt and remembered. The writing of those words excavated things he thought were long buried. They gave him back himself. Sharing them was a gift of trust. In the safe place we created in our correspondence, I put words to feelings I had never admitted before.

Dear Daniel,
Sometimes people ask me why I don't have children. I'm always appalled at how people can ask that, since it is so personal, and where would I start? I say something like "it wasn't in the cards" and smile, but inside I feel sad. And, as I've been writing to you, I've seen patterns in my life that eluded me before. I was young, awake, in love with the idea of love, and then it all shut down.

I had cancer of the uterus. It was found after years of excruciating pain and many misdiagnoses. It explained why I couldn't get pregnant after many attempts. I know this sounds crazy, but I think sometimes illness comes from emotional trauma. There is a story I haven't told you.

It has been three years since Japan, three years since Pete and I broke up, and still no one can compare to him. Pete haunts my dreams and longing for him fills my notebooks. I've told my friend Teri about him. We met waitressing at Smitty's Pancake House and became fast friends. After she left for California, she sent me a postcard inviting me to come. I have decided to join her on the first leg of my journey to find Pete.

I have a plan. I will write to Zazie, who is living with a Japanese family in Kyoto, and tell her I'll meet her there, after I've saved money from waitressing in California and Hawaii along the way.

Japan. My mind floods with images. I picture all the different ways I might run into Pete: at his favourite coffee shop in Kobe, or on the streets of Kyoto. He will look at me with disbelief, grab me in his arms, put his fingers to my lips and say "Shh," before kissing me the way he used to.

In his embrace, I will find myself again.

Teri is staying with a bunch of surfers in a beach house near Encinitas. I move in and find a job waitressing in a smoothie bar. The ocean tides wash away the cold university years, and the California sun turns my skin brown. In the evenings we sit and watch the sun fall below the waves, listening to the Eagles. I think, *That is Japan, right over there, where the sun is going down.*

After six months Teri and I move on to Hawaii—one step closer. We find lodgings at a hostel near the University of Hawaii at Manoa, and Teri gets work carving candles in an outdoor market in Waikiki. I find a job greeting Japanese tourists at the airport, handing out leis and taking their pictures, and a second job waitressing in a Mexican restaurant at night. The tips are good and my travel fund is growing, almost enough for the flight to Osaka and extra to live on when I get there. I'm anxious to get to Japan but enjoying the adventure, the beach and the laid-back Hawaiian rhythm.

A bartender I work with is one of the best surfers in Hawaii. He tells stories about surfing before dawn: the roar of an approaching wave in the darkness, intuiting the swell, paddling furiously to get on top of its ridge, then riding through as the sun rises. Hawaii is full of surfer boys. When you ask "How are you doing?" they answer, "*Da kine.*" That is the Samoan phrase for the big one, the good one—the best ride.

One day I take a shower at the youth hostel, leaving my sundress, the one I wore on the first day of school at CA, the one that once belonged to my great-aunt Helen, on a hook. It's gone when I come out of the shower. Who would steal it? I know most of the girls and they all seem nice, but one is a thief, and she has stolen something that mattered to me. I'm really upset.

"Can I borrow something to wear to work?" I ask Teri.

× × ×

That night we are short-staffed and I have to work later than usual. When I finish, I consider going to one of the big hotels that line Waikiki to get a taxi, but it's an expensive fare to Manoa.

I'm waiting at the bus stop when a car pulls up. Two guys who look like surfers ask if I need a ride.

"No. Thanks."

"There won't be another bus tonight."

I look at the schedule, right there on the signpost. The last bus was at eleven-thirty and it's now quarter to twelve. Damn. The hostel is way up the road. I climb in the backseat of the car, thinking of the taxi money I am saving.

The guy in the passenger seat has long blond hair, which is why I thought they were surfers. But once inside, I notice his hair is greasy. The car reeks of cigarettes and weed.

"I'll drop my friend first," the driver says. I can't really see his face. He pulls up at an apartment block. They both get out. "I'll be right back," the driver says. "I'm just picking something up."

I fidget, waiting in the car.

He returns with what looks like a folded cloth. "Okay, I'll take you to the hostel. Get in the front seat."

As we drive, I ask him about different beaches and the best waves, parroting things I've heard in the bar, talk any surfer would pick up on. He barely answers.

He takes Kapiolani Boulevard, passing University Avenue.

"Hey, you missed my turn." I don't know Honolulu well, but I know the turn for the hostel.

He accelerates and takes the next turn, the ramp onto Highway One.

A knot in my stomach starts to feel like a fist. "Why aren't you answering me?"

"Shut up."

We are flying along the highway now. Mind racing, I wonder if I can jump out. I imagine asphalt meeting bare skin. Maybe he'll get off the highway, maybe we'll hit a red light and I can jump out and run. He grinds his butt into the ashtray, pulls off the highway and down a road somewhere above the valley, to an overhang. He cuts the engine. It's pitch dark.

"What are you doing?"

He reaches for something down the side of his seat, maybe the cloth he picked up at his friend's place. It looks like a dishrag. Then the glint of the blade.

This is how it happens, I think. *This is how stupid girls die.*

"Stop screaming." He yanks a fistful of hair, pulling me close to the blade. My right arm tries to reach the car door, and he smashes my head into the side window.

The heel of his hand is pushing against my mouth. I writhe, I scratch, I bite.

"Bitch."

He tears at my skirt. It's the one I've borrowed from Teri, pale yellow with flowers. *Don't ruin the skirt*, I think irrationally.

His fingers claw at my thighs, poking and jamming, tearing down my underpants.

"NO. NO. Stop!" It's the last day of my period, and I'm wearing a tampon just in case.

His hostility turns to rage. "Fuck you, bitch!"

"I'm on my period. Please. Stop. You don't want to have sex." A last attempt, as if talking to a rational person.

His fist slams into my cheekbone. He yanks on the string of the tampon and it scrapes out dry, burning my insides.

No. I stiffen and make my body a board.

He presses the knife to my throat. "Feel that?" His sweat smells strange and rancid. I can't breathe with the blade against my windpipe. He jams himself inside me. I've left my body and am suspended above.

When he finishes, he takes his hand from my mouth. I gag at the disgusting smell of his come.

Sirens. Headlights turn everything to white.

"If you say anything, I'll kill you."

A flashlight shines in his face. "Please step out of the car."

Three police cruisers surround us. They pull him out, spread him across the hood and handcuff him.

A police officer opens my door. I am slumped against the passenger seat, head down, face behind hanging hair.

"Did he hurt you? There were calls to 911 from several houses in the valley below, reporting screams coming from up here," the cop says.

I say, "He threw the knife over there."

Fluorescent lights scorch my eyes. Someone brings me a blanket. They help me onto a table, spread my legs and put me in stirrups and scrape my insides. They give me the morning-after pill. Detectives and rape counsellors want to ask questions. I want to close my eyes.

They bag my clothes, Teri's skirt, as evidence. Someone gives me something to wear. Just before dawn a detective drives me to the hostel.

Everyone is sleeping. I creep into the room, climb into the lower bunk and curl up in the fetal position, smeared with his filth, soiled and shaking and broken, waiting until the shower room opens in the morning.

Teri gives up her work shift to stay with me. Since the hostel is closed during the day, we take a bus to the far side of the island. On the blistering sand, under the tropical sun, covered with a towel, I shake so hard my knees knock, unable to get warm.

A few days later I am called to the front desk of the hostel. It's the detective.

"He's gone," the detective says.

"What do you mean? I saw him taken away in the police cruiser."

"They let him go."

He looks angry, apologetic. "He couldn't be held for more than forty-eight hours without a grand jury indictment, and it was the weekend. We got the indictment Monday morning. He was gone when we went to arrest him."

I have no words.

"We have issued a statewide alert. If you leave Hawaii, please tell us. You are the primary witness."

"Witness?" I think of myself suspended above the scene, witnessing what was being done to a young woman who thought she was going to die.

"Rape is a felony A and a crime against the state."

My parents beg me to come home but I tell them I need to wait until they find him; I want to stay for the trial. Teri and I find a sublet near the university. I write to Zazie, tell her what happened, that my trip to Japan is delayed.

I see him. In different places, in crowds, across the street. But maybe it's not him. He haunts my dreams, deprives me of sleep.

"This is normal," the rape counsellor tells me. "You are processing."

"I thought he would kill me."

"The good thing is, you are alive."

One day his friend, the one in the car, is on the street walking towards me. I'm positive it's him. Does he know what happened? Did he know what would happen that night? I run in the other direction until my lungs explode, then stop, put my hands on my knees and vomit.

Zazie writes in shock and concern. *Go home. This is not the time for Japan. Besides, it's not the Japan you remember.*

At the bottom, scrawled as an afterthought, or perhaps to bury the hurt she knows it will cause, she adds:

P.S. I ran into Richard, Pete's brother, and guess what??? Pete is married with a baby, living in Nashville, Tennessee. Maybe your destiny is not as close as you

thought, or maybe you will meet again in ten years in Omoto, land of the beautiful.

The ink bleeds, smudging the words. Words erasing hope, words that have made it final. Pete is married. I've lost the one I love. I've lost my faith in the legal system that was supposed to protect me. I've lost my faith in men.

I don't wait any longer. When the plane lifts and the islands of sunshine disappear beneath the clouds, I think of the roar of a big wave approaching—the one you can't see in the dark.

One evening, a car slows down while I'm walking to my parents' house.

"Hey, babe."

I walk faster. There are guys hanging out the car window, clearly drunk.

"Hey, you, come and get some."

Tears drip down the back of my throat, bilious oil floats in my belly.

"Hey, stuck-up bitch."

When I get home, sobbing and slightly hysterical, my mother takes me to task. "You can't go on being afraid of your shadow."

"I want justice," I tell her.

She is a social worker. She doesn't mince words. "No one gets justice."

I volunteer at the rape crisis centre to fight the feeling that rape will always stalk me. Still, it finds me everywhere, especially in the bedroom. When I try to have sex, my body locks in self-defence. For years I just get stoned and pretend.

× × ×

The college-age girl who lives next door to my house in Toronto is making love. I can hear her through the walls of my study in the afternoon, when her father is at work. Her moans grow louder until she screams in climax. I want to pound on the wall and shout "Stop!"

In the months since Daniel died, I've been excavating my past, looking for the truth—or the lies I told myself—in the faded pages of my journals. Did I really always love him? How did I manage to forget? Who was that young woman who came back from Hawaii, the woman who got married a few years later to someone from the music industry she met at a party? "I can't believe you married someone in the music biz," Daniel wrote years later. "You were in my world!"

But I wasn't. I hated the scene, the come-ons, the late nights in bars that smelled of stale beer. I preferred to stay home and read a book. I was in another world, trying to be a wife, when it still hurt to be touched.

I open another journal and a letter falls out, dated three months after the rape, written to my future self. I have no memory of writing it. In it I promise to "live fearlessly." *Fearless* is the biggest word when you're frightened all the time.

The girl on the other side of the wall screams again in climax. This time I cheer her on.

× × ×

The phone rings. "This is the prosecutor's office of Honolulu."

The person on the phone informs me that the man who raped me has been arrested in Texas. He is wanted by several states, but my case is the first. Will I come back for a trial? If so, they will extradite him to Hawaii.

My boss at the film company where I've started work gives me time off, but says, "I don't think you should go. The trial might be worse than the event." *How could anyone think that?* I fume. Nothing could be worse. Nothing could be worse than letting a rapist walk.

I am twenty-three years old; I have moved in with the man who will become my husband and I'm employed by my future lover. I'm hardworking, eager and smiling, but stone-cold inside. When things get bad, I take out the cardboard folder I keep hidden. Inside are photos of Japan: misty landscapes and thatched-roof farmhouses, rocks, trees, rice paddies, my friends, pictures of me sitting at my desk peering over my glasses, or with hands in jean pockets, looking off into the distance, two passport-size photographs of Pete, and the picture of us on a train.

I have my airline ticket and am packing to leave when another call comes through. "I don't know how to tell you this," says the assistant DA. "The evidence box has gone missing."

Teri's pale yellow skirt, the tampon, the knife, the rape kit—vanished. How can that be true?

"We no longer have enough evidence to extradite him. Don't worry; he will stand trial in Texas. You weren't the only one, just the first one. He won't get out of prison in this lifetime."

Simmering rage now reaches a boil. If they hadn't released him before the grand jury met, those other women would have been spared.

I travelled the world and collected first-hand accounts from women whose stories had never been told before. I wrote a book called *Women in War*; made a documentary called *No Man's Land*, about women journalists covering war; then *Rape: A Crime of War*, on the rape camps in Bosnia, and *Crimes of Honour*, documenting femicide in the Middle East. After many years and many films, a divorce, an affair, and a million miles circling the globe, came the pain. It woke me at night.

I paced the floor until I was so exhausted I fell asleep, but the deep, cold pain woke me again before dawn. I saw specialists, took prescription drugs, had experimental surgery, but the pain grew worse, until they told me I needed to have my uterus removed.

In the recovery room the surgeon told me he'd removed my ovaries too, because I had the worst infection he'd ever seen. I was home from the hospital when he phoned with the pathology results. "Thank god we took out the ovaries," he said. I had been riddled with cancer.

× × ×

Dear Daniel,

It means so much to be able to write to you about this. I don't tell people. I don't dwell on it.

Writing it down felt like a surge of river water in spring after the ice has melted, but ice had kept me strong. Now I was vulnerable.

Dear Shelley,

I am shaken by what you told me and what a ride you've had. I don't know what to say. I can say this: I think that emotional trauma is frequently the direct cause of illness. I also think that it works both ways; in other words, a cure or healing can be affected through the same agency. I am so impressed, so warmed by the karmic balance you've created with your life and career, transmuting your experience in such a transcendent way.

He wrote at length about my film *Rape: A Crime of War.* He understood why I needed to tell these stories. He went on to describe the deep feelings he was experiencing—feelings, he wrote, that had never ended.

With his words, I started to heal.

Morning

Good morning, dearest Shelley,
There's nothing you could say or do that's going to affect what we have now. There's nothing you could say or do that would change the love I feel. I have all the same questions; is it just a recap of what we had, a nice dream of the past? Is it a hungry response from someone (me) that has been so long without this kind of love? I can go on and on about what it might be, but I do know in my heart of hearts what it is.

I love you, Shelley. I wish I could whisper it in your ear. No matter what happens in the near future, no matter how long it takes, I hope we will find out about this love and what shape it will take in our lives.

I wasn't expecting this to happen, but it has. I've been absolutely overwhelmed by this love and I can't find the right places to put everything—I opened the door and there you were, flooding my heart, everything different, everything lighter, brighter, and a chance to know you again.

This has to be the most terrifying email I have ever sent.

All my love,

Daniel

The Circle

DAWN FINALLY ARRIVED, ending the longest night. I dressed in the clothes I'd laid out on a chair: jeans and a Gap turtleneck the colour of salmon, carefully chosen to look unintentional. How would I appear to him? What would he see when he laid eyes on me after so long?

I waited by the front door next to my suitcase, feeling a little nauseated. I checked my bag for the hundredth time—yes, there's my ticket, my passport, and my reading glasses.

Kirsten pulled up outside and honked lightly. I bent down and petted Alley Cat and Dylan, who were swirling their tails around my ankles, and hugged Deborah, who'd moved in with me after her breakup and would keep editing our film while I was gone. She, like all my friends, was expectant for me.

"I'm so excited for you, Shell. Have a great time. Don't worry about anything here."

I shook my head at the audacity of it all: setting off to spend a week with someone I had not seen in three decades. I told her, "I might be back in a day."

Kirsten drove me to the airport and handed me a Valium. We laughed at the irony. I'd flown to some of the world's most dangerous places and never taken a Valium before a flight.

"It will be okay. Remember, you are just meeting an old friend," she said. We both knew I wanted more.

Changing planes at O'Hare in Chicago, I almost turned back. What if we fell flat? What if we fell further than that? But we had grown so close over the past seven months, sharing the most intimate stories of our lives, acknowledging the depth of old feelings and tiptoeing around new ones. We had waited months while he restored his health and body. It was time. I popped the Valium and boarded the plane for Salt Lake City.

Crammed in the last row of coach, I tried to get comfortable. I opened a book, but the words floated off the page. The expanse above the clouds seemed endless, as though time itself were suspended. I pictured the plane stationary in the sky, a white bird in a child's drawing. Three hours would close the gap of three decades, but no flight had ever felt so long.

In need of a distraction, I relitigated the story I had always told myself, summarizing its content, revising with new information.

All those years ago, when I learned that Pete had married, I thought he had found "the one." That meant it had never been me. I pictured him holding a woman, holding a baby, imagining an epic romance. But the story he eventually told me was different.

He'd gone to Nashville hoping for his big break, and when it finally came, with an offer to join Dolly Parton's band on tour, he rushed back to the house of the woman he'd been staying with, eager to pack and share his news. She had news of her own.

> Pregnant???? We didn't have any kind of relationship, based on interests or communication. I considered myself a temporary houseguest. But there she was claiming maternity to my paternity. I was 19 years old. I'd never felt so alone. I ran a bath until it was scalding hot, climbed in and cried.

He got married and found a job in an auto-bumper processing factory. He tried to be a father to his infant son, but the marriage was mired in resentment and lasted only two years. By the time I received Zazie's letter in Hawaii, telling me he was married, it was already over.

The flight attendant handed me a coffee. Outside the plane window, everything was white.

> After my marriage there was a vigorously promiscuous period where I reveled in my freedom. But every relationship usually involved guilt (on my part) when I was off making music instead of spending time with a girlfriend, or resentment because I had made the choice to spend time with a girlfriend instead of doing what I wanted to be doing.

> Incessant demands for reassurance, insincere compromises, and always, ALWAYS communication levels would reach their maximum depth level, and it just wasn't enough. The points of reference just weren't there.

I sipped my coffee and took a long look at myself. Would I have been able to handle Pete any better? In Japan our relationship was intense, intimate, complete. I never had to compete with his music. Would I have gone with him on the bus, sat with the groupies and other band members' wives?

I had stood on my own two legs for so long: independent both financially and professionally. I had started my own company, bought my own home. Yet if I had known he was divorced when I left Hawaii, everything might have been different.

I tried to picture it: I'd have gone to Nashville and found him. In my imaginings, soon I'd be pregnant with his babies, making homemade soup, telling him I didn't mind when he left to jam all night or went on the road for months. We'd have rented an old house with two cats in the yard, just like the Graham Nash song. I'd have been the woman he wanted to come home to.

But what would my life have been like? What would I have done with the fire inside me, the issues that burned, the injustices I wanted to shine a light on? Would loving him have been enough to replace the drive to make documentaries, the camaraderie and challenges of filming on location, the heady feeling that always accompanied the big "get"? I'd never made a pie in my life; I buy soup at the store. I wish I'd had his babies, though. Our kids would have been phenomenal.

Pete eventually owned seventy guitars, became a studio session player and played "fixes" on albums for some of the greats, but his own big break never came back around. After another, much longer failed marriage, he left behind the music scene and even the name Pete. He went on the road, this time working on restoration projects. He was in Salt Lake City restoring the governor's mansion when he decided to stay for a while. "Why Salt Lake? Why not?" he wrote. He'd been coasting, waiting for something, and had finally settled for what was. His son was in his twenties now. He regretted that they had become distant.

I thought of the boy I had loved in Japan, the one full of hope for the future. Life had brought disappointments. Was our second chance coming too late?

The pilot announced our descent. I closed the unread book in my lap and put away my reading glasses. We landed, and soon the aisle was a wall of people jostling oversized carry-on bags and winter coats. There wasn't enough air on the plane. Clawing at my turtleneck, waiting for the doors to open, I felt faint. When the line finally began to snake forward, my legs felt unsteady.

Inside the terminal I looked for a restroom to check my face and run a comb through my hair, but there was a lineup there too. Unable to take the suspense any longer, I began to run. Through the endless terminal, along the moving sidewalk, almost bumping into people, I ran until I saw a man waving at me.

He didn't seem familiar. Daniel had not sent me a photograph, but I was sure I would know him. My pace slowed, my heart pounding in my ears. I didn't recognize him at all. This was a terrible mistake.

I stopped for a moment, unsure what to do, and then a woman moved in front of me and ran into his arms. When they cleared my frame of sight, there was Daniel, leaning against the Arrivals wall, hands in his pockets, grinning.

I would have known him anywhere.

"Pete . . . Daniel . . . I . . ."

"Shh." He put his finger to his lips. "Don't speak."

He opened his arms. "Come here."

We sat in the bar of a posh hotel, drinking each other in. My beautiful long-haired boy was gone. The man who sat across from me had classic male pattern baldness and a beard flecked with silver. His face was chiselled by manhood. There were lines around his eyes, which changed colour from grey to green to fawn, just as I remembered. He had become even more handsome. I couldn't stop staring, couldn't stop smiling, couldn't stop shaking my head.

Daniel ordered a single-malt Scotch for himself and vodka for me, and then we fell silent. After the mountain of words we had exchanged for seven months, we found ourselves nearly speechless.

"My god . . ."

"I know . . ."

There it was, the sexy crease in his cheek when he laughed. I began laughing too.

Later, at his favourite sushi place, we found our voices. He told me he had been so nervous on the drive to the airport he hadn't properly closed the hood of his car, and it flew open on the highway, almost causing an accident. I confessed I had nearly turned back in Chicago.

The chef spoke to Daniel in Japanese.

"He asked about you and I told him a little."

"*Omedetō gozaimasu*," he congratulated us, with a bow.

We walked back to the hotel where Daniel had booked a suite, wanting our first night to be on neutral ground. "I can sleep on the couch," he said.

He took some candles from his overnight bag and opened a bottle of wine. Then he handed me a package.

I pulled at the string, careful not to tear the handmade paper. Inside was a yukata the colour of lilacs, with traces of white branches and blossoms. A memory surfaced: a kimono slipping from one shoulder, his lips brushing my skin.

I smoothed the folded cloth. "It's so beautiful. Thank you." I met his eyes, erasing all the nights in between.

"I have something for you too." I handed him a sweater of soft grey-brown wool with a small leather logo sewn on. I usually detest logos, but I had chosen the gift because of this one. Roots, a Canadian company, used the year of its inception to brand its products: 1973.

I knew exactly where my lips would touch his chest when he pulled me to standing. I knew his taste when he bent his head for a kiss.

He undressed me slowly and said, "You are mine."

"Let go for me," he whispered, and I let go.

Afterwards, we lay facing each other. I traced the line of his cheekbone. It was more than chemistry, more even than love. I knew him as I knew myself.

We slept like children, curled close, without dreams. We had imprinted at seventeen. Together we were whole.

I woke to an empty bed and the sound of a door opening.

Daniel came in, fully dressed, holding two cups of coffee. "Good morning."

I rubbed my eyes to make sure he was real, sat up like a princess propped by pillows and reached for the cup.

Later, while I ran my fingers across his chest, he told me about the mountain he had climbed, the weight he had lost, the pain he had endured to heal his feet and restore his body, all in seven months. "You made me a man again," he said.

The November sun hit the mountains with a cool, crisp light. We drove a little out of town and pulled into a place called Ruth's Diner.

"This is my favourite breakfast place," he said. I wanted to know all his favourite things.

Suddenly I was ravenous. The waitress came by with the coffee and called us both "honey."

"Perfect moment," I said.

× × ×

On the way to Park City, a ski town in the Wasatch Mountains, famous as the home of the Sundance Film Festival, we stopped for groceries. Pushing the cart through the aisles, greedy with happiness, we grabbed anything we wanted: decadent and lovely things, packages of olives and Brie, smoked salmon, grapes, chocolate, wine.

Later we strolled through the town. The sky was a deep Prussian blue, dotted with billowing clouds, but the air was cold. Daniel was stomping the pavement in the cowboy boots he still wore and blowing on his hands.

"Let's get a drink and some dinner," he said, and grabbed my hand the way he used to. My heart swooped and soared like a bird.

Our glow was infectious. Servers smiled. Customers at the next table smiled. Sitting next to a roaring fire, we fell again into disbelief.

As we left the restaurant, streaks of orange and violet slashed the sky. It was as though everything beautiful was being refracted and multiplied. Daniel ran ahead, his arms reaching for the colours. Above him, the streetlight illuminated a few dancing flakes.

"Look, it's snowing!" I called.

I wanted to stay outside in the snowfall; wanted to be inside, buried in his arms. I spun and twirled in the street, making him laugh. I wanted everything at once.

Later he lit a fire in the place we'd rented and picked up

his acoustic guitar to strum a Crosby, Stills & Nash song. A pang of nostalgia and regret swept through me. But as suddenly as the feeling came, it lifted. *This* was the time I'd been waiting for.

It is said we become different people every seven years, changing down to the molecular level. If that is true, Daniel and I had become different people four times over since we were last together. In some ways everything about him felt new. He had become measured where I was too quick, careful and exact where I was impatient. He sipped his Scotch slowly while I gulped down a beer. He had learned to love jazz, the difficult kind. I still craved the beat of rock 'n' roll. But we each slid into the same side of the bed as we had in Japan, and still lit each other up with a single touch.

"Marry me," he said on day three. It wasn't a question.

"Yes. Yes. Yes."

River Stone

THREE WEEKS AFTER our reunion in Utah, Daniel came to Toronto for Christmas. I introduced him to Alley and Dylan, my cats, and to my closest friends. We decorated a tree, lit the fire, cooked, made love and watched the snow fall.

On Christmas Eve we paid a visit to Ed.

My friend was lying in a hospital bed in the dining room of his home, no longer able to move. I was shocked by the change in him. When I had seen him before I went to Utah, four weeks earlier, he was still in a wheelchair. I had booked him a series of home massages as a surprise gift before I left.

Daniel clasped his hand, then moved off to give us a bit of privacy. He knew that Ed was one of my dearest friends and that we had shared a pining for our high-school loves.

"I'm so glad you found each other," Ed whispered to me.

My eyes filled with tears. I reached down to kiss him, knowing it was goodbye.

"And thank you for finding Kathy."

I thought I had misheard, or that he was delirious on

end-of-life drugs. But when we were leaving, his sister walked us to the door and told us a story.

A massage therapist had shown up at the house, Snaige said. "She was tall, with long, wavy dark hair, and looked exactly like Ed's first love. And here's the strangest thing, Shell. She said her name was Kathy."

On Christmas morning Daniel and I sat amid a mountain of opened gifts.

"No more," I protested when he handed me another.

"This is the last one."

I untied the ribbon and unwrapped the homemade paper, revealing a river stone. I picked it up, feeling its surface worn smooth by the river tide.

He answered my unspoken question. "From Kochi. I've had it since I was a boy."

He'd had Japanese kanji carved on it.

"What does it say?"

"*True love.*"

It fit perfectly in the palm of my hand.

It has been ten months since Daniel died. The last of winter, the filthy piles of blackened snow and ice, has finally melted. I call my cousin Lynne and suggest an outing. I've been inside too long.

We decide to see Yoko Ono's new show, *The Riverbed.* I'm startled to find that the city is regaining its colour. Buds are popping out from every branch and bush, almost fluorescent green in their newness. The sky is an impossible shade of blue.

The gallery rooms are almost entirely white. In some places white is the colour of rebirth. In some places it is the colour of mourning.

We enter a room and read Yoko's instructions: *Take a piece of broken white pottery, make something, glue it to a piece of string and place it on the wall.* The gallery walls are a montage of fluxion. I sit at a table and try to think what to make with my shards. A jagged heart, a broken wing? The walls seem to speak with a thousand voices, murmurs and whispers emanating from each creation in white.

Zazie once told me that Yoko still had John's white piano. "It's the first thing you see when you enter her apartment in the Dakota," she said.

Seven months after I'd placed my wish on Yoko's tree, five months after Zazie's wedding, Daniel and I lay entwined, marvelling at fate. He had held me while I sobbed at Ed's funeral, and we comforted each other when we learned of the death of Eddie Kanai in Kobe—Eddie, who had been one of our *nakōdo*s, our matchmakers.

We visited California that spring and spent the summer in the Wasatch Mountains. We went to Mexico and splashed in the dazzling sunlit waves, and in the fall visited Daniel's parents in the Blue Ridge Mountains of North Carolina. (His mother remembered me as "the girl from Beijing" and his father as "the Canadian girl.")

We went to British Columbia to visit mine. My father, who had already apologized to Daniel over the phone for "that awful time in Toronto," shook his hand and handed him a single-malt Scotch. On the terrace overlooking orchards and the blue lakes of the Okanagan, my mom looked at us and summed up the way I felt. "It feels like you've been together for thirty years."

Daniel designed our wedding bands and carried them in his pocket, but life kept delaying our plans. We wanted a wedding in Japan, though friends and loved ones were spread across the globe and we were still living in two countries. Daniel had projects as far afield as Nigeria, while I returned to Iraq in May 2003, soon after the American invasion, to try to find the children we'd met before the war, and then I began a documentary in Hebron, on the West Bank. We saw each other when we could and ached at each parting.

The wedding kept getting postponed. We had it all, but in darker moments I wondered if we were squandering it. Love had come around again, so why was I on a plane to Tel Aviv?

"If this were a novel, I'd throw the book away," I said one night on the phone. "Twenty-nine years apart and now deadlines and work and immigration laws separate us?"

He said, "I'm catching the next flight to Toronto."

We walked into Toronto's City Hall on a windy Friday night in November, exactly two years after our reunion in Utah. The elevator opened at the appropriate floor and we stepped into a hallway strewn with bales of carpet awaiting installation. A man reading a newspaper pointed us down the hall. We entered a room with a few rows of chairs and some dusty dried flowers.

I welled up. This was hardly the wedding I had dreamed of. "Maybe we should leave," I whispered.

Kirsten and Susan, our witnesses, bounced in, phones set to video. Behind them was the officiant, a tall man with an infectious smile.

"Daniel and Shelley? Are you ready?"

I looked at Daniel. He took my breath away, tall and handsome in a black jacket. I smoothed down the velvet dress I had found in a vintage store and fingered the necklace of garnets and gold that Daniel had clasped around my neck.

Yes.

The officiant began with a quote from Emily Dickinson, and the ugly civic room was transformed. The shot was a close-up, the background blurred, lit with the glow of rightness.

Daniel took the rings from his pocket. They were braided strands of rose, yellow and white gold, "For past, present and future," he said. We slipped them on each other's fingers.

Sipping French champagne late into the night at an extravagant bistro with Kirsten and Susan, we talked about the next chapter. Daniel had to return to the States—the civil ceremony hadn't really changed a thing. But it had. I was *married* to the person I had always loved. What could be better than that?

We chose to make Toronto our home. Daniel loved its large Asian community and felt that his roots in the States were tenuous. When his immigration papers finally came through, we began the life we'd always wanted. We cooked together, took walks in the park, slurped noodles in Chinatown, and shared our angst over life's challenges. We hung out with friends. We watched the news, celebrated special times and sometimes nothing at all, laughed every day, painted the kitchen, and planted a rose garden. We entered into sleep together. We embraced every morning.

Sometimes I would pick up the river stone with the characters for true love just to feel its weight in my hand.

I asked Daniel to make me two promises right from the beginning. "Never walk away from me again. Stay and fight, even if I make you crazy." The second was "Please, quit smoking." He kept the first and tried his best with the second.

It has been fifteen years since I placed my wish on Yoko Ono's tree. Layers of time seem to haunt this gallery of white. I wander into the next room. A bed of stones has been placed on the floor, winding to form a river. Some of the stones have words carved on them. *Peace. Forgive.*

I sit on one of the meditation pillows to think. Daniel gave me a river stone at our first Christmas, long ago. I wonder if a word or expression carved into stone is something intrinsically Japanese or just a random coincidence. How did I find myself here in all this blinding white? I reach for a stone that says *Remember.*

Stone to stone, circle within circle, connecting the river of life.

Notebook

THE SIGN SAYS in Japanese: "Take your own photos, four different poses."

Pete and I are downtown in Sannomiya after school. We want photos to give each other. Pete puts a hundred-yen coin in the slot and climbs into the booth behind a red curtain.

Flash.

The light from the camera is blinding. Pete isn't ready, or maybe he's goofing around. He holds up his jacket as if to shield his face from the light. His eyes are downcast and his lashes fall to his cheekbone, face half hidden in profile. The corner of his mouth is curled with a hint of a smile. His long hair is tucked behind his ear and there is a glint from his gold hoop earring. You can see the veins and muscles of his left hand, the light illuminating the tip of his wrist bone.

The three other poses from the photo strip are lost but I have hung on to this one. I'd hidden it away for decades, until I dug it out to show friends after finding Daniel again. "You can't really see him, but it captures him completely."

Susan had it enlarged from passport size and framed it for me. She and Kirsten took many pictures of us on our wedding night, capturing what felt like a miracle. We celebrated the fact that, in the end, destiny had not abandoned us. A thousand seemingly random choices had led us on different paths and then brought us back together. Everything was finally, exactly right.

Kirsten and Susan broke up years ago, but after Daniel's diagnosis, Kirsten made a difficult phone call. She asked Susan if they could get together to make a gift for me.

"I'm not sure if this was a good idea." Kirsten was nervous when I tore off the wrapping paper. There was Pete, in the photo-booth picture, his image gracing a coffee mug and the covers of ten spiral notebooks.

"Oh, so sweet . . ." I stammered, not knowing what to feel.

"I took a gamble," Kirsten said.

I wasn't sure what Daniel would make of it when I showed him the gift later.

"I'll take a notebook, but you keep the mug," he said, smiling. "It's a bit much for me."

The mug sits on my desk, holding my pens, and the notebooks are almost filled. I open one, hardly recognizing my handwriting.

Exam room at Princess Margaret . . . Daniel's sleeping on my coat, rolled up like a pillow. The past four days have been like this: exhaustion, seizures . . . so much pain. What do you give someone going through this? Love. Today it doesn't feel like it's enough.

My right ear begins to throb against my jawbone.

No one tells you this: Losing the person you love is the same as losing yourself. You spend your days searching for memories to moor yourself to, but involuntary memory is something else. It crashes in on waves of grief without warning.

Flash.

It's Valentine's Day, just after a dinner that Daniel hasn't been able to eat. The phone rings. It's Mary Ellen. She and Ann, Daniel's two older sisters, often call me to hear how he's *really* doing before talking to him.

This time when I say hello, she asks me to pass the phone to her brother. He listens quietly, turning even paler than before.

When he hangs up, he tells me the news. Mary Ellen has pancreatic cancer. His sweet, beautiful sister, who hikes and jogs and has never smoked a day in her life. Mary Ellen lives in D.C., where we cried together just a few months ago while she helped me pack up Daniel's condo.

How can this be happening? First, my brother-in-law James, then Daniel, and now Mary Ellen, all diagnosed with late-stage cancer.

Five weeks later, Ann calls. Mary Ellen is dead.

Flash.

It's May. My dad is in St. Mike's Hospital. My mom calls me early in the morning and my sister Trish and I rush to Emergency. It's gallbladder disease, requiring surgery. But on the operating table the anesthesiologist discovers an embolism in his lung. Things go really wrong from there.

Trish and I take shifts, spotting each other so each of us can get home to be with our ill husbands. When my dad's stomach stops working, we call my brother in Hong Kong. My mom, who has dementia, keeps asking "Why is everyone dying?"

I get home one night, throw in the laundry and sit down next to Daniel in front of the TV. There's a whining sound, followed by violent shaking. Our washing machine gives up the ghost with a very loud bang.

"It's the Book of Job," Daniel says, and despite it all, we helplessly fall about laughing.

On the tenth day my dad rallies. He's discharged from hospital with a tube in his stomach connected to a drainage bag. When I get home, I find Daniel rocking back and forth, holding his jaw in his hand, sobbing, in excruciating pain. He'd been fine when I left in the morning.

It's Sunday night; I can only reach the hospital hotline. I write in my notebook: *Extreme pain in right jaw. Spoke to doctor, told me to give him extra hydromorphone, 2 x 2 mg as needed until we can get to the hospital.*

Flash.

I am holding Daniel's arm as he makes his way down the three steps to the street and into a cab. I've bought him a cane at Shoppers Drug Mart, and he is using it for the first time. It's awkward getting into the low backseat, and the cane tumbles to the floor of the car. The cab drops us off a block from the entrance of Princess Margaret Cancer Centre because of all the construction. Impatient drivers honk behind us.

We make it through the scaffolding and broken concrete to the main entrance, to the elevator banks, up to the fourteenth floor, looking for the sign for Palliative Care. Daniel is white as a sheet by the time we get there. He wants to lie down. He slumps against me in the waiting room.

I skim the notebook I've been keeping, so I can tell the doctors what I've seen in the past twelve hours: *Word and memory loss. Didn't remember where I'd gone. Seizures. Hallucinations. Says his sister is in our house.*

In the doctor's office, Daniel stretches out on the examination table and drifts off. There's a doctor, a resident and a specialty nurse.

"Do you have home care?" one of them asks me.

"No. No one has told us we could—"

She cuts me off. "We can put in a request. When was his last bowel movement?"

"Not for a few days. It's the meds, and really, he isn't eating. It might be longer."

"A week? That could be the trouble. You need to give him an enema."

I'm not sure how this would cause jaw pain or the mixing up of words or the hallucinations, but at this point I'm looking for a miracle. "Do you really think it could be that?"

"Yes. Go to the pharmacy and buy a Fleet enema. Do it today."

"Okay, yes, but what else? I mean, what should we do? He can't climb stairs anymore and he doesn't eat and it's hard to get him to swallow his pills."

"See you in a week."

A week? The team stands as one, holding their clipboards, indicating that our time is over. I've learned that the Ontario health-care system is based on fifteen-minute appointments. If your session goes on longer, you are cutting into someone else's time.

"But—"

The medical team is gone. A ping comes from my phone. The Princess Margaret hub portal shows an appointment at four p.m. It is only eleven in the morning, but there isn't time to go home and come back to the hospital. I can't think straight. We were here until midnight the night before, waiting for an MRI. Daniel threw up several times.

In the waiting room of the Lung Clinic, Daniel sleeps in his chair, slumped against me. I read emails on my phone and play Candy Crush. Four hours and thirty minutes pass.

Someone calls, "Peterson."

The radiation doctor seems elated. "The MRI is clear; your brain is fine. Phew, you had me really worried. I didn't think the brain radiation caused the pain in your jaw, but now I can rest assured. But . . . we do have some bad news. Your CT scan shows that cancer has spread to your liver. Unfortunately, there is nothing more I can do. Do you have any questions, sir?"

Sir? He has always called Daniel by his first name. From somewhere deep inside himself, Daniel comes back into the room and asks, "Where do we go from here?"

"I told you, there is nothing more I can do."

I hate him. This nice man who was so kind when we first met now won't look me in the eye. I hate him for calling Daniel "sir." I hate him until he throws us a bone.

"I see you have an appointment with your oncologist next week. Maybe she will offer more treatment."

But how can I get him to his next appointment? How can I get him upstairs to bed? How can I get him to swallow pills, the only thing saving him from pain? I already know, in my heart, that his body can't tolerate more chemo.

At five a.m. the next morning I sit in his blue chair and write a group email to his friends.

> Daniel can't talk on the phone anymore; I know some of you have been trying. If you want to say something, please put it in an email and I will read it to him.

My coffee tastes salty from the tears falling into the cup.

An email drops. It's from a friend, sending a link to a local hospice. I click on it, knowing what the doctors won't tell us: I can't save him this time.

My hand is resting on the notebook. I study each black dot that makes up his image, trace the line of his brow. It soothes me to look at his face, even if half hidden. How is it possible that I won't see him again?

My mind takes refuge in the past, and I go back to the beginning.

There is Pete, complete and reckless with youth, Pete

with blood coursing through his veins. He's on the beach in Kochi, where the ocean and rivers meet, sitting cross-legged, as he always does, staring at the sea. The sun has dropped low on the waves, its light slanting across the side of his face, then hitting the tip of his wrist bone.

The Photograph

IT HAS BEEN eleven months since Daniel died.

I'm in the Hamptons with Zazie. After two cancelled trips, I've finally made it to see her, wanting to find what is left of myself, as one can do only with a very, very dear friend. We walk along the deserted beach and talk about the present. We sip tea and I listen as she weighs some decisions about the future. We sit cross-legged on her wooden floor in shafts of light, poring over her journals of our time in Japan.

There are ink drawings and bits and pieces glued onto the pages: a flyer for *The Crucible*, with all our names listed in the cast, next to a sketch of a teapot.

"We seemed to smoke a lot of hash." She laughs, pointing at one entry, then another. We fall back into time.

"Look at all Mark Ashida's photographs. He was your *nakōdo*," she says, using the Japanese word for bridge or matchmaker.

"It wasn't Mark," I reply, "but he took our picture—the one of Pete and me on the train."

I feel lighter than I have for months, finally able to laugh. I wake early and look at all the shades of the ocean, calling me back to life. Beckoning me from the blue.

"If the house was burning, what would you save?" I once asked Daniel.

"Our photograph," he replied, without pausing.

"Right answer."

He had driven a U-Haul across the States, packed with his art books and guitars and treasures from his boyhood in Japan and his mother's childhood in China. When we set up our home, we married our lifetime of collectables, placing the samurai sword-guards Daniel had collected at Kochi Castle as a boy next to the silver candlestick I'd bought in a deserted Palestinian shop on Martyr Street during the second intifada. But of all our totems and possessions, it was the photograph we treasured the most.

"It's a miracle you kept it," Daniel said.

"That's why you had to marry me."

That photograph, taken on a train to Hiroshima at the end of our trip to Kochi, rests in a chipped Victorian frame. After we married, we hung it in our bedroom, where our younger selves stared back with teenage eyes. They couldn't see the future, but the photograph witnessed everything that had lain ahead: the hunger and desire in intimate moments, the sleepy bedside murmurs, two bodies nestled close, eyes waking to the sun or rain or snow. It witnessed conversations on the phone when geography separated us and we talked about everything—the news of the world, the day that lay ahead, challenges at work, meals we would cook, friends we would see, places we wanted to visit. It witnessed us collapsing in laughter over any stupid thing. It watched us traverse twelve and a half years of married life: the minutiae and the boring, the stressful and the miraculous.

Our photograph witnessed the morning I collapsed after the night in Emergency when we learned his diagnosis. It watched as we lay in the dark after he came home from the hospital a few weeks later. *We'll face this together*, we told each other. We didn't yet know how disease would try to separate us: I wasn't the sick one and couldn't absorb his pain. Fear threatened to divide us, too. I couldn't admit how dark it was getting. When Daniel tried to tell me, I wouldn't listen.

"Go to sleep, baby," I said one night when he started to talk about dying. "In the morning things will feel different." I'd developed a serious case of denial. He was unable to eat more than a few bites, saying everything tasted of ash. His digestive system was messed up from all the narcotics. He could no longer write or type because of tremor in his hands. He didn't have the stamina to go for walks, so we'd cross the street and sit on a park bench to watch dogs run and children play and birds hop.

"Is everyone looking at me?" he asked when people walked by.

"No. Why do you ask?"

"I think I already look dead."

I shook my head and told him the truth: he still looked beautiful to me. But I was fighting a dark depression and working hard to hide it. My mental state had manifested in a series of nervous tics. My eyes were glassy from anti-anxiety pills, and I'd started pulling out my hair.

"Why do you keep scratching and rubbing the top of your head?" he asked, looking across the room at me.

"I do?"

"You do it all the time."

At the hospital I filled out the questionnaires for him sometimes a little too quickly.

"Why did you give me a score of 9 out of 10 on depression?"

"Well, I thought—"

"I think you're answering this for yourself. And here—you answered 'high' on the question of sexual concerns. Great. Now the nurse will have a heyday with me."

A few days later I got up my nerve. We were sitting in the living room in our usual spots. "How can you not be depressed?" I ventured carefully.

"Depression is a state of being, a condition," he answered. "I feel sad. This is incredibly sad, but that's different from existing in a state of depression." Trust Daniel to mark the difference.

Every third week we woke at six a.m. and headed to the hospital. After blood work to determine his white cell count, he'd spend four hours in a chemo chair, three days in a row. First a bag of saline, then two different bags of poisons, while other patients came and went. Nurses sometimes shook their heads at the killer dose he was getting.

Our pharmacy bills were piling up; one set of injections alone cost $1,700. I was managing our money, watching the war chest of our combined savings dwindle. Neither of us was working, and planning ahead was impossible.

One morning after the rounds of chemo had ended—after six months of brutal, debilitating treatments that left him so weak he either fell to the ground or lurched from his chair and clung to the mantel—I woke up and looked at our photograph. Daniel needed a lift. What could I do?

The idea arrived with utter clarity. I sprang out of bed and walked over to the photo, touching his teenage nose with my finger. "I'm going to surprise you."

When Daniel got up, I handed him his morning coffee. "Do you feel well enough to go to Long & McQuade music store?"

He looked at me with astonishment.

"I think we should get that guitar you love."

"But we can't afford it."

"Yes, we can," I lied.

When we'd gone to buy guitar strings a few months earlier, Daniel had fallen in love with a Fender Telecaster the colour of butter. "It's amazing," he'd said, eyes wide as a child's. He and the salesman swapped stories while I perched on a stool, watching. "It's a great axe, with a really thin neck. Easy to get your fingers around."

I glanced at the price tag and gasped. It was over three thousand dollars.

For weeks after that, he'd read online reviews. "It was Keith Richards' favourite," he'd say. Or "Look what Jimmy Page is holding!" His other guitars were now too hard for him to hold. This one would wipe out our savings, but I no longer cared.

We entered the store and asked for the yellow Fender hanging on the wall. Daniel's face was pale, his eyebrows and eyelashes gone. A grey hat covered his completely bare scalp and he walked very slowly. His hands shook, either from the treatments or from the disease.

The salesman brought him a stool and placed the guitar in his hands. As soon as Daniel held it, his tremors stopped. His face was flushed with happiness.

He named her Buttercup. From then on she was in his arms or perched next to his chair from the moment he got up each morning. He played her almost without stopping. He played along to the CNN news and as an underscore to Netflix dramas.

"Are you sure it doesn't bother you?" he'd ask.

"No, don't stop. I love it."

Music filled our house; chords and combinations flew from his fingers. It wasn't the rock or folk or bluegrass he used to play. These were strange and wondrous improvisations. He told me, "I've never played like this before. I don't know where it's coming from."

But I knew. It was music unfettered by ambition, free of self-doubt. He was not playing for an audience. He was in tune with a deeper rhythm.

Music pushed fear into the background. I started to picture a different future, one in which a miracle might happen. Maybe we could rent a cottage for the summer, or drive to California.

"Maybe I'll record some of it," Daniel said.

"The soundtrack for my next film," I added. I could feel the music healing us, but it also opened a psychic door. Past ghosts began to enter.

"I've made so many mistakes," he started one night, just as I was drifting to sleep. This was the time he usually picked to say things that demanded attention.

"I left you and I left music. Why did I let go of the things I loved?"

"But you got them back," I whispered.

"I know, and I don't want to leave you."

His sleeping pill kicked in before I could find the right words to respond. His breathing relaxed into sleep, while I lay awake in the dark.

Our photograph bore witness to it all. A few weeks later, paramedics carried him downstairs and into an ambulance. Buttercup was leaning against his chair.

It is coming up to a year since he died. I begin to empty cupboards and clean floors, trying for a fresh start. I put on some music, wanting to fill these rooms again with sound. Running a duster over the furniture, I move and sway to the rhythm. I gently dust his guitars: Buttercup, the red Fender Stratocaster he played onstage, and an electric guitar he built himself. They sit in their stands, red, yellow and red, all in a row.

The Chicks' "Bitter End" comes on the playlist and stops me in my tracks. It's a song about lost friends, about someone who should have played on.

Buttercup's surface is shiny, almost brand new. For the first time I notice that Daniel had placed a pick behind the strings at the bridge, waiting to be used.

Tears that haven't come for months, suppressed tears that blocked my sinuses, now pool in my eyes and blur the room. There's an ocean roar in my head—a dike has been breached. Tears fill my ears and nostrils and the back of my throat, making me sputter and choke, making it hard to breathe.

I'm on my knees by his guitar. The torrent bends me in two. I weep until my stomach hurts and my head crashes and there's nothing more.

Natalie is still singing, asking the question I always ask: *Where'd you go?*

I stumble upstairs and into our bedroom, staggering towards the curtains, wanting to block the light.

There he is, on the wall by the window. He's holding the hand of my younger self, our entwined fingers just out of frame. I stare into his eyes, still so alive. He looks back at me and smiles.

When the Light Broke

"TELL ME I'M beautiful, one more time."

"So beautiful," he said and then closed his eyes. I knew that no one saw me as he did. I needed to hear those words from him again, one more time, to last me.

I had managed to get him downstairs, and we were sitting on the white sofa in our living room. I stared ahead, my eyes resting on the wooden bodhisattva from a Kyoto temple that had been our wedding gift from Zazie. Daniel had named him Curly, for his bald head. He stood three feet high and held a crystal ball in his outstretched hand. The last sunlight of the day was making patterns on Curly, dancing silhouettes of leaves and branches. I watched, transfixed, for what seemed like hours, holding Daniel's hand as he drifted in another realm.

The patterns of light swam and blurred as my eyes filled and clouded. Daniel was leaving. I couldn't hold him much longer.

"Just one more question, please, baby. I know you're tired."

He heard me and opened his eyes.

"Can we do this again?"

He looked at me and smiled. "Yes," he said. "Absolutely."

We had posed this question—more a declaration—to each other countless times before. It was a nod to our interrupted love story, a nod to second chances.

"We'll do it again, only better," Daniel always said. "Next time we'll never be apart. Next time we will have children."

The light played on, flicking and flashing. "You are so beautiful," I whispered. No one else would ever make my eyes as happy. No one else would read my mind the way he did. No one else would hold my heart in their hands.

The room took on an unearthly light; the day was almost gone. Daniel was leaving. He could swallow no more pills; there was no food to prepare. There was no moment but this one.

I touched his lips with mine. His breath, which had mingled with mine in a thousand kisses, was becoming weightless on its sacred passage to next time.

I wake early and stumble downstairs. The clock on the stove says five a.m. The first shafts of light make patterns on the grass. Sparrows are swooping low and landing, pecking at bugs and worms. The weather is cool, with the promise of a warming sun. Tiny pink rosebuds emerge from woody stalks; the garden is about to explode. The terracotta pots are still empty and the garden neglected, but our little paradise is trying to tout its beauty.

Today is the one-year anniversary of Daniel's death. I place my hand on the counter to steady myself against the swell. Pour a cup of coffee and go sit in his blue chair.

Morning after morning I'd wake to the aroma of brewed coffee, would stumble downstairs and into his arms. "Morning, beautiful," he would say, handing me a cup.

I take a sip of my bitter brew, wondering how I made it so strong. I lean my forehead against my hand.

It was five a.m. when the neurosurgeon came through the curtain and told us Daniel had lung cancer. It was five a.m. when I went to find the hospice nurse ten months later.

"He's moaning. I promised him no more pain."

The nurse held his hand, feeling his pulse. She turned to me. "He's leaving. Are you ready?"

"I'm ready," I answered, knowing her meaning. "But . . . could I hold him?"

She gently pulled on the underpad beneath him, moving him over a bit to make a little room, and helped me climb in. She brought me a pillow and said goodbye. "I won't see you again."

Our bodies nestled close. I held his hand and listened to his breath slipping in and out. We stayed like that for hours, travelling the in-between world, until the light came.

I murmured words I hoped he would hear. "I've got you. I will always love you. You can let go."

The garden has emerged from the darkness. The first of the roses he planted have opened overnight. Some say a year is the marker, that then the time of grieving is done. But there is a chasm that has grown ever wider, and a shadow where I used to be. It is five in the morning, the beginning of another day and another year. How do I find my way back?

Mountain

MY BROTHER JIM and his husband, Keith, have done all they can. They've cooked for me, poured me gin and tonics, sat up late to keep me company in the library of their farmhouse in Tuscany, left me alone to read or sleep during the day, or coaxed me out on long bike rides through sunflower fields. Some days we explore the different towns dotting the landscape, savouring the *dolce vita* of an Italian summer. I smile and sip my *caffè latte* while watching people in the square, a little glassy-eyed, as though seeing everything from under water. Jim and Keith might have exchanged worried looks, but they've never let on. It's true; I'm still not myself.

I was afraid to return to Italy because it was here, in their home, that I got the phone call from Daniel. I think of that call as a demarcation line. Before, when things were almost perfect, and after.

It's been fourteen months since Daniel died, and my friends and family are worried. I haven't sprung back to life as they'd hoped. A trip might be the cure. Jim and Keith coaxed, my parents bought me a ticket and my sister Trish got upset when, a few days before my departure, I said I couldn't go, that I didn't want to leave her when her husband, James, was at death's door.

Two sisters with husbands diagnosed with stage IV cancer at almost the same time—what are the odds? Trish said, "The only thing that is making me happy is the idea of you getting away." She didn't want me to face any more hospital rooms, and I didn't want to upset her, so I got on the plane.

After two weeks in the healing sun, in a place where joy of life is bred in the bone, I begin to feel something stirring inside me. Jim and Keith have to leave, to return to their other lives, but I've decided to stay on in Italy.

We load the car with food: ripe tomatoes from the vines, figs and pasta sauce, bottles of gin and wine, and some warm clothes in case the weather turns. Drive forty minutes through the countryside, filling up water bottles, stocking up at a Co-op grocery store and buying a few things at an outdoor flea market, then head up the winding road to arrive at Montone, a medieval village nestled in the Apennines where my brother has a tiny flat.

We hug goodbye.

I shut the door and fight down a moment of panic. I don't have a car, don't speak Italian, and there's no internet in the flat. I look around: a wooden table to write on, a shelf lined with books left by visitors over the years, some old CDs, and firewood stacked next to the fireplace. I pull out a white brocade bedcover we found at the flea market and place it over the old brown sofa. Better—not so dark and forlorn. To warm up the tile floor, I lay down a threadbare carpet I found in a trunk. I unpack bags of food and candles, books and notebooks, pens, paint and canvas. This feels like a monastic cell, a self-imposed exile. After so much time alone this past year, why have I chosen this solitude? I climb into the narrow bed, pull the covers over my head and sink into oblivion.

Church bells peal, counting eight. Can this be eight in the morning? It's the first night in more than a year that I have slept through. Rubbing sleep from my eyes, I put on Jim's old terrycloth robe with the Armani label, a remnant of our carefree youthful days of fashion and excess, edge my bare feet into hotel slippers I nabbed in Rome, walk into the main room and pull open the heavy wooden shutters. Outside, rooftops glow golden orange against the mountains. I catch my breath at the sight.

Lighting the gas flame, I make an espresso and step outside.

I've brought bright geraniums to cheer up the terrace and begin filling cracked terracotta pots that held nothing but weeds. I sweep away the dirt and clip the blooming hedge that lines the outer terrace, which sits atop a Roman wall. Below is a deep drop; at the bottom I see small shapes of children entering a school on the road directly below. I edge backwards, almost stepping on a scorpion, which scurries into a crevice in the stones. I find the hose under the stairwell and spray everything down, cooling and calming, soothing and reclaiming. My task is slow and certain. The fears of last night wash away with the water and are thrown out with the weeds.

At the small, round table, I open my computer and notebooks. This is why I have come. Fingers rest on the keyboard; eyes close in a moment of prayer, waiting for the first word.

Faint voices echo from the valley below and become louder. The mountain is bathed in sunlight that has burned through the morning mist. Is that him walking up the mountain road? My heart begins to sing at the thought of the day ahead. Maybe today he will notice me. Pete has come back to school.

The clock on the wall must be wrong. Have five hours really passed? I haven't moved from this chair. A surge of energy flows through my veins.

Come on, let's hike down the mountain and explore.

I look up and smile. He takes my hand and unlocks the front door.

I've been writing our story as I remember it. Spending days, nights, weeks alone on a mountain with my love. He has been here with me, hiking every path down to near the field of horses, over past the olive groves, and back up to sit and rest at one of the three tables at the bakery, smiling at the old lady who sells linens in the courtyard, watching a stray cat sleep in the sun. To some I might appear to be a woman alone.

I have gathered every sliver of memory imprinted on me. Listened for fragments of long-ago conversations, echoes of laughter, moments of joy. I've scanned for images emerging from the mist. I've written everything down.

Now the wind has come up. It was sudden; the morning was hot and sultry but, as if to signal that my time here is ending, a tempest is beginning to blow. The skies are moving rapidly; white and blue patches quickly subsumed by clouds of pewter grey. The air brings a vapour chill; my bare feet feel cold against the tile floor. The endless summer is turning.

Yesterday, as I was lying in the sun, a daydream came. Behind closed eyelids, the golden light suffused a scene of happiness. It marked the beginning of *want*. To want something again lifted me from the place of emptiness.

Daniel would understand the ache, the chasm that will never fill. But he would not want me to fall into it and disappear. He would laugh when I admit that grief, above all else, becomes boring.

It's time to leave. The muscles in my thighs and calves have become stronger from hiking up and down the mountain paths every day. My eyes are clear from feasting on olive and lemon groves and a thousand shades of natural beauty. I have shed skin, sloughed it off with every move I made. I've conquered my fear of solitude, of being alone with loss.

The window shutters bang shut. Dogs bark in the distance, heeding the change in the air. A great wall of sound, like the roar of the ocean, is circling closer; it pulls away, then rushes back. The storm is coming in.

Tonight I will hunker down in this aerie perched on the edge of a Roman wall, where every house is built to weather these storms. People long dead carved this village out of stone, plastered walls thick and hammered wooden shutters onto windows that opened to the sun and closed to the bitter elements. They built monuments of grandeur such as the cathedral up the road, out of scale in this tiny place and yet . . . why not? Why not build something beautiful and epic and lasting? Why not say *Throw at us what you will, we will survive and overreach our smallness.*

Daniel would have loved the frescoes and the vaulted ceilings. He would have known the kind of paint they used, how they mixed it to make the textures and tones. He would have known what lay beneath the broken colours. We would have sat together looking in awe, the way he taught me. But Daniel never got here. This is my place to be alone.

The valley grows dark. Tonight I'll light a fire, and when I wake, it will be time to go home.

My bags are packed and ready, sitting by the door. The flat is polished clean, the windows and doors shuttered. I've put all the perishables out with the garbage and folded everything neatly away.

It's cold out. The winds last night swept away the last of summer. It's time to return to a life where people need me.

But I'm not quite ready. There's something in the furthest recesses of my mind. Something I need to remember. Something I need to write down.

One more memory, please.

From behind scudding clouds I see it: a glowing orb trying to break through.

"Look," Pete says, pointing at the full moon. We are standing on the mountain ridge overlooking Kobe, which lies like a necklace of sparkling gems below.

It is late. Night fell hours ago. Pete has brought me back to campus after curfew, but we aren't ready to say goodnight.

The lights at the entrance to the girls' dorm have been switched off. The window to my bedroom on the far side is dark. It's warm, almost summer. A swell of cicadas rises and falls.

Pete drapes an arm around me. I rest my head on his shoulder, circling an arm low around his back, hooking my fingers into his jeans pocket.

We don't speak. We don't kiss.

We watch the miracle of the night sky spread out before us. In it we see a future filled with possibility, but we already know that no moment will be more perfect than this one.

Whatever happens, whatever comes.

Acknowledgements

TO WRITE ACKNOWLEDGEMENTS for a story that encompasses the arc of my life is daunting. So many dear friends and colleagues have taken parts of this journey with me. Whether named or unnamed in these pages, you have each been a treasure to me.

To all my classmates and teachers at the Canadian Academy in Kobe, Japan, thank you for being part of an unforgettable time and place. Especially Alexandra Munroe; Mark Ashida, whose photograph of Pete and me still hangs on my bedroom wall; my dear roommate, Celia Oyler; confidantes Brenda Tenorio and Yvonne Pearson; and favourite teacher John Low. Thank you, Gregg Johnson, wherever you are, and the late Eddie Kanai and Mary Enloe for being our *nakōdos*, our matchmakers. It makes me smile to imagine Daniel hanging out with Eddie and Mary in some celestial bar, listening to rock 'n' roll.

All my life I've been lucky in my choice of friends. Many became part of a family of talented journalists and filmmakers who have worked together with me: Deborah Parks, Deborah Palloway, Kirsten Scollie, Cristina Senjug, Cornelia Principe, Michael Grippo, Peter Sawade, Lyse Doucet and Olivia Ward. Thank you for sharing so much of my story.

When I started writing this memoir, in bits and pieces as fragmented as my heart at the time, several angels appeared. Marina Nemat's *Prisoner of Tehran* was sitting next to me on my bookshelf when I chanced to see a Facebook ad for her memoir-writing course at the University of Toronto. Marina, your class was the thing that gave me purpose after Daniel died. I can never thank you enough for your brilliance and generosity as a teacher.

Debi Goodwin showed up at my door with flowers from her garden and, having recently lost her own husband, became my companion through grief. Among other acts of kindness, she invited me to join her writing group, which became a touchstone as I struggled to put together the pieces of random scribbles, journal entries, emails and memories to tell this story. Thank you, Debi, and all the remarkable and gifted writers in our "dear cru"—Janet Looker, Jamie Zeppa, Maria Cioni, Maria Coletta McLean and Barbara Tran—for your friendship and advice and for giving me the courage to keep writing.

Kyo Maclear suggested Kendra Ward as an early draft editor, and Kendra's sensitive, thoughtful notes helped guide me forward. Thank you to both these amazing women.

Talent and literary agent Perry Zimel is someone I could always turn to for help, from the earliest days of my career. He enlisted the great Kate Nelligan and the legendary Christopher Plummer to narrate my films. When I asked him for advice on publishing my memoir, he first told me how difficult it would be, then asked me what it was about. I said, it's a love story. Luckily for me, Perry is also a romantic. He read it in one night and is now my agent! Perry, thank you so much for your belief, enthusiasm and tireless championing of this book.

My early reader group kept growing. Some offered suggestions, made corrections or posed questions. All encouraged me, just when I needed it most. Enormous thanks to these dear friends: Brenda Morgan, whose colour-coded annotations were incredibly astute and so helpful; Alexandra Munroe, who, among other things, corrected my Japanese; my beloved late Lindsay Knight, who helped me puzzle out the timelines; dearest "other one" Olivia Ward, whose *Toronto Star* stories about Daniel gave his work to the world; and Kirsten Scollie, for seeing me through the worst and always believing in me. Thank you to new friends Sharon and Susan Okun, Adam Markovic, Regina and Bruce Robb, Candace Maclean and Alison Fardoe, and to lifelong friends Teri Leese and Greg and Karen Zelonka. Thank you to Jodey Porter for our walks and conversations, to Anne Bayin for the inspiration, and to the amazing Mellissa Fung, who became one of the book's most ardent advocates and connected me with Jamie Broadhurst. Thank you for your love and support.

Above all, my undying gratitude to Anna Maria Tremonti and John Filion, who demanded two copies so they could read side by side on their holiday! They cheered me on, read it more than once, and after John corrected some of my music references, asked if he could send it to his friend and editor, the legendary Anne Collins, executive editor at Random House Canada. John's persistence got my manuscript into the hands of the person I most wanted to read it.

In many ways I have lived a blessed life. But few moments have been more exciting than when Anne Collins called me to say she had read the manuscript. Thank you, Anne, for your belief in the book, which changed everything. I can't believe I've been lucky enough to work with you. Your compassion, sensitivity, perceptiveness and deft touch have made every page better. And thank you to Susan Kuruvilla, publisher of Random House Canada, who championed the book along with Anne and, in some mysterious design of fate, shares with me a life-altering sojourn in Kobe, Japan. You both made my publishing dream come true.

To Daniel's family, the Petersons, and especially to his sister Ann, who is the keeper of this family's extraordinary history and was with me in Daniel's final days, my heartfelt gratitude. And when it comes to my own family, who have been my rock through everything, there isn't a big enough word to express my love and thanks. If my mom, Jane Saywell, could read this, no doubt she would add some counsel or tease me about taking myself too seriously. She always said just the right thing to keep us humble! To my incredible father, William, and the best siblings in the world, my brother James and sister Trish—who also lost her husband,

James—thank you for listening and reading early drafts and giving me advice and affirmation. You have each inspired me countless times over a lifetime and have always been there when I needed you. Along with my brother-in-law, Keith, and nephews Mack and Tom, you are my heart and foundation.

To my brilliant friend, my beloved Zazie, Alexandra Munroe, thank you for confirming my memories and sharing the best of them. From the first day of school to this day, you have been my chosen comrade and shining light. So much of this story is yours too.

And finally, to Daniel Peterson. Daniel. Pete. Loving you has been the greatest joy of my life. Thank you for the words you sent that first brought hope and later solace. Sharing them makes this book ours. Our story, our love. Nothing could be better than that.

Shelley Saywell is a Canadian documentary filmmaker and author. Her first book, *Women in War: Firsthand Accounts from World War II to El Salvador*, gave a voice to women who had never told their stories before. Then she began filmmaking, bearing witness from some of the world's most desperate places. Saywell has written, directed and produced more than twenty independent documentary films, telling stories of struggle and conflict, the fight for justice and the power of hope. Her films, including *A Child's Century of War*, *Kim's Story*, *Out of the Fire* and *Martyr Street*, have been shown in more than thirty countries and won numerous awards, including an Emmy for investigative journalism. Saywell has been personally honoured with the WIFT Creative Excellence Award and a UNESCO Gandhi Medal for the promotion of peace. Her memoir, *If Only Love*, is the story of the great love and events that shaped her life behind the lens.